Building Grade 5 SPELLING Skills Daily Practice

What's in This Book?

This 30-unit book contains strategies and practice for learning 540 spelling words.

Each unit contains:

- a list of 18 spelling words
- two sentences for dictation
- four activity pages for practicing the spelling words

Words on the spelling lists were selected from:

- a list of the 600 most commonly used words in English
- words frequently misspelled by fifth-graders
- words with common phonetic elements
- words changed by adding prefixes and suffixes and by forming compound words and contractions

Additional resources:

- "How to Study" chart
- "Spelling Strategies" chart
- forms for testing and recordkeeping

Correlated to State Standards

Visit *www.teaching-standards.com* to view a correlation of this book's activities to your state's standards. This is a free service.

 EMC 2709
Evan-Moor®
EDUCATIONAL PUBLISHERS
Helping Children Learn since 1979

Author: Jo Ellen Moore
Editor: Leslie Sorg
Copy Editor: Cathy Harber
Illustrator: Jim Palmer
Desktop: Jia-Fang Eubanks
Yuki Meyer

Contents

Teaching the Weekly Unit

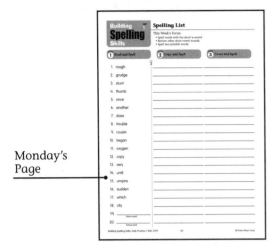

Monday's Page

Strengthening Students' Spelling Skills

Spelling Strategies
Page 6

How to Study Your List
Page 7

At the beginning of the year, reproduce pages 6 and 7 for each student or on an overhead transparency. Review the general steps and strategies, encouraging students to apply them throughout the year.

Monday

Allot ample class time each Monday for introducing the spelling list and having students complete the first page of the unit.

Introducing the Week's Words

Give each student the spelling list for the week. Here are ways to introduce the words:

- Call attention to important consistencies noted in "This Week's Focus," such as a phonetic or structural element. For example, say: *As we read this week's spelling list, notice that all the words have the same vowel sound.*

- Read each word aloud and have students repeat it.

- Provide a model sentence using the word. Have several students give their own sentences.

- If desired, add "bonus words" based on the needs of your class. These may be high-utility words or words that the class is encountering in curricular studies.

Writing the Words

After introducing the words, have students study and write the words on the first page of the unit, following these steps:

Step 1: Read and Spell
Have students read the word and spell it aloud.

Step 2: Copy and Spell
Tell students to copy the word onto the first blank line and spell it again, touching each letter as it is spoken.

Step 3: Cover and Spell
Have students fold the paper along the fold line to cover the spelling words so that only the last column shows. Then have students write the word from memory.

Step 4: Uncover and Check
Tell students to open the paper and check the spelling. Students should touch each letter of the word as they spell it aloud.

Home Connection

Send home a copy of the Parent Letter (page 145) and the Take-Home Spelling List for the week (pages 10–19).

Tuesday — Word Meaning and Dictation

Have students complete the Word Meaning activity on the second page of the unit. Then use the dictation sentences on pages 8 and 9 to guide students through "My Spelling Dictation." Follow these steps:

1. Ask students to listen to the complete sentence as you read it.

2. Say the sentence in phrases, repeating each phrase one time clearly. Have students repeat the phrase.

3. Wait as students write the phrase.

4. When the whole sentence has been written, read it again, having students touch each word as you say it.

Wednesday — Word Study Activities

Have students complete the activities on the third page of the unit. Depending on students' abilities, these activities may be completed as a group or independently.

Thursday — Edit for Spelling Activities

Have students complete the activities on the fourth page. Depending on students' abilities, these activities may be completed as a group or independently.

Friday — Weekly Test

Friday provides students the chance to take the final test and to retake the dictation they did on Tuesday. A reproducible test form is provided on page 142. After the test, students can record their score on the "My Spelling Record" form (page 141).

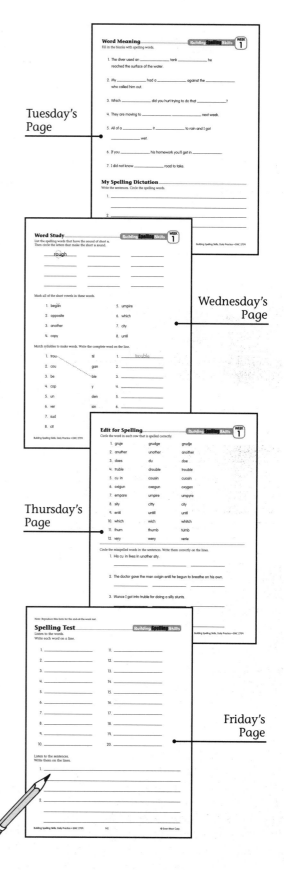

Tuesday's Page

Wednesday's Page

Thursday's Page

Friday's Page

Spelling Strategies

Say a word correctly.

- Don't leave out or mispronounce sounds.
- Write the sounds in the correct order.

Think about what the word looks like.

- Think about how the spelling pattern looks.
- Write it, look at it, and decide if it looks correct.

Look for small words in spelling words.

- spin—**pin**, **in**
- cupcake—**cup**, **cake**

Look at syllables in spelling words.

- Spell the word one syllable at a time.
  remember—**re** • **mem** • **ber**

Use rhyming words to help spell a word.

- If you can spell **book**, you can spell **look**.

Use rules for adding endings.

- Drop the silent **e** before adding a suffix.
- Double the final consonant before adding a suffix.
- Change the final **y** to **i** and add **es**.

Use knowledge of prefixes and suffixes.

- Think about what the word looks like without the prefix or suffix.
- Write the word and then add the prefix or suffix.

These strategies help me become a better speller!

6

How to Study Your List

① Read and Spell

② Copy and Spell

③ Cover and Spell

④ Uncover and Check

Good for me!

Sentences for Dictation

There are two dictation sentences for each spelling list. Space for sentence dictation is provided on Tuesday of each week and on Friday's test form (page 142).

- Ask students to listen to the complete sentence as you read it.
- Have students repeat the sentence.
- Read the sentence in phrases, repeating each phrase one time clearly.
- Have students repeat the phrase.
- Allow time for students to write the phrase.
- Read the sentence again, having students touch each word as you say it.

Week Dictation Sentences

1 The **stunt** diver used an **oxygen** tank **until** he reached the surface.
All of a **sudden** my **cousin** was in **trouble** with the **umpire**.

2 The workers **laid** a **straight** track for the **freight** train.
They listen to their **favorite radio station** at **daybreak**.

3 Player number **fifteen** was **eager** to hear the **referee's** decision.
She was **ready** to buy that **unusual** stone **cube**.

4 Is the sailor's **goal** to set sail on the **ocean tomorrow**?
He **followed** the **oldest** man but didn't **approach** him.

5 **Who's** going to collect the six **o'clock** mail when **it's** delivered?
Doesn't he know **they've** already discovered **whose** purse it is?

6 I found **myself smiling** at the funny **rhyme** about a **knight**.
Where do you **apply** to **buy** a fishing **license**?

7 Kids in my **neighborhood usually choose** to play after **school**.
You **should** be sure to read the **bulletin Tuesday** morning.

8 It was our **choice** to climb the **mountain** by **ourselves**.
Somehow one **ounce** of **oysters** doesn't seem like the right **amount**.

9 In **high school everybody** learned **something** about **first aid**.
Is it **all right** to send **everyone's birthday** cards by **airmail**?

10 Was it his **fault** that the **awkward** dancer took an **awful** fall?
The **author always brought** his work to the editor's **office**.

11 The **tiniest** lady **carried** her own luggage while **traveling**.
Both boys **laughed** as they **finished trading** silly riddles.

12 Do you have the **addresses** of your **friends** in other **countries**?
One of his **businesses** is taking **pictures** of **families**.

13 What was the **purpose** of the **mayor's** speech **early Thursday**?
The **smuggler** was selling a **camera** for only one **dollar**.

Week Dictation Sentences

14 An **important article** about **dairy** cows came out in **January**.
Why was the police **force guarding** the **orchestra** conductor?

15 A **thousand different animals** live **along** the **equator**.
Dr. Hill gave his **second lecture** on treating **puncture** wounds.

16 How many **children** made **purchases** of **chocolate** this **month**?
I **thought** I would **exchange** my gold **watches** for **white** boots.

17 **Since** the flood, people have been **generous** with their time and money.
Is it **peaceful** or **dangerous** in that **country**?

18 I have a **question** about the **address** on that **label**.
There was a **special** sale on **towels** for a **whole** week.

19 King Harry **hurried** his plan to defend the castle from a **fierce siege**.
Neither worker is **receiving** a **piece** of the profit.

20 The **biologist's assistant** worked **speedily**.
My **teacher** was filled with **loneliness** and **sadness**.

21 Mr. Lee's **heir** spent the money she received on **clothes** and a **cruise**.
He **knew** the length of each king's **reign** since the Middle Ages.

22 Through **skillful** negotiations, the **government** was **successful** in reaching a solution.
Did their **reckless** behavior deserve such a harsh **punishment**?

23 The **musician** was **sure** that hard work and **patience** would pay off.
His **official mission** was to map the **position** of **glaciers**.

24 The boys will pack **knapsacks** and camp on the **island tonight**.
Listen instead of **talking**, or you will give the **wrong answer**.

25 You'll have to **rewrite** the story if your handwriting is **illegible**.
Father will **disapprove** if we **misbehave** or are **dishonest**.

26 The **roughest physical** activity was on the **fourth** day.
A **fragile** girl went to the **pharmacy** for **cough** medicine.

27 Was he **unaware** that his **improper** behavior made us **uncomfortable**?
They were **uncertain** how to **prevent prejudice**.

28 The **geologist's autobiography** seemed as long as an **encyclopedia**.
She used an **automobile** to **transport** her largest **photographs**.

29 Pay **attention** to her **description** of the fire's **destruction**.
Why are they going to **divide** the **administration** into two parts?

30 Do **amphibians** live in an **environment** with a low **temperature**?
Early **civilizations** developed **agriculture** and the use of **currency**.

Building Spelling Skills

rough

grudge

stunt

thumb

once

another

does

trouble

cousin

began

oxygen

copy

very

until

umpire

sudden

which

city

_____
bonus word

_____
bonus word

Building Spelling Skills

afraid

explain

payment

sleigh

laid

raise

straight

freight

height

they

favorite

April

able

radio

station

relation

daybreak

trace

_____
bonus word

_____
bonus word

Building Spelling Skills

fifteen

referee

eager

easily

ready

please

ecology

maybe

been

only

universe

future

communicate

beautiful

unusual

cute

cube

fuel

_____
bonus word

_____
bonus word

Week 4	Week 5	Week 6
obey	I'll	idea
ocean	they've	silent
poem	don't	myself
echo	we're	lying
hello	didn't	apply
wrote	isn't	knight
goal	couldn't	quite
approach	haven't	I'm
owner	o'clock	license
tomorrow	you're	buy
program	who's	inquire
broken	whose	higher
potato	aren't	variety
throat	it's	smiling
oldest	doesn't	diagram
followed	there's	rhyme
spoken	won't	widest
awoke	I've	python

cut

cut

_____
bonus word

_____
bonus word

_____
bonus word

_____
bonus word

_____
bonus word

_____
bonus word

gloomy

school

choose

loose

route

clue

truth

duty

ruin

Tuesday

usually

threw

understood

neighborhood

rookie

could

should

bulletin

_____
bonus word

_____
bonus word

spoil

choice

avoid

moisture

oyster

royal

employ

annoy

ground

house

sprout

mountain

allow

ourselves

somehow

ounce

amount

boundary

_____
bonus word

_____
bonus word

cut

baby-sit

first aid

flashlight

high school

goalkeeper

all right

airmail

one-way

bodyguard

something

good-bye

birthday

outside

everybody

everyone

anything

themselves

himself

_____
bonus word

_____
bonus word

cut

Building Spelling Skills

stalk

off

because

brought

called

drawn

awful

awkward

lawyer

daughter

fault

author

always

already

although

belong

office

haul

bonus word

bonus word

Building Spelling Skills

surrounded

skiing

swimming

loving

studied

traveling

carried

trading

bragged

worried

beginning

exciting

finished

laughed

quickest

weaker

tiniest

lonelier

bonus word

bonus word

Building Spelling Skills

countries

addresses

women

lessons

people

skis

friends

roofs

calves

fences

flies

lives

cherries

businesses

guesses

families

leaves

pictures

bonus word

bonus word

cut

Building Spelling Skills

NAME

WEEK 13

urgent

Thursday

purpose

thirsty

camera

wonder

smuggler

remember

surprise

earth

certain

person

dollar

color

collar

early

mayor

doctor

_____

bonus word

_____

bonus word

Building Spelling Skills

NAME

WEEK 14

square

stare

dairy

area

January

dictionary

daring

beware

argument

large

partner

guarding

article

orchestra

ordinary

important

force

before

_____

bonus word

_____

bonus word

Building Spelling Skills

NAME

WEEK 15

about

algebra

quiet

other

compare

thousand

happen

different

along

equator

dozen

animal

second

region

quarter

lecture

puncture

again

_____

bonus word

_____

bonus word

cut

cut

Building Spelling Skills WEEK 16	Building Spelling Skills WEEK 17	Building Spelling Skills WEEK 18
NAME	NAME	NAME

Week 16	Week 17	Week 18
awhile	signal	eagle
where	regular	example
thought	generous	towel
athletes	energy	special
truthful	bridge	legal
purchases	genius	little
exchange	dangerous	whole
though	segment	several
rhythm	figure	terrible
children	country	label
chocolates	circle	question
friendship	concert	frequent
together	peaceful	telescope
white	nice	instead
watches	since	instrument
arithmetic	electric	celebrate
months	dancing	declare
length	decided	address

cut

cut

_____
bonus word

_____
bonus word

_____
bonus word

_____
bonus word

_____
bonus word

_____
bonus word

© Evan-Moor Corp. • EMC 2709

© Evan-Moor Corp. • EMC 2709

© Evan-Moor Corp. • EMC 2709

tried

weigh

piece

receive

their

fierce

neither

field

receiving

trying

hurried

siege

weighs

writing

tired

having

planned

worries

bonus word

bonus word

kindness

darkness

happiness

loneliness

sadness

weakness

exactly

honestly

speedily

angrily

happily

friendly

especially

teacher

actor

liar

biologist

assistant

bonus word

bonus word

scene

they're

through

heir

clothes

byte

aloud

cruise

crews

isle

principal

principle

hour

knew

two

write

chute

reign

bonus word

bonus word

cut

cut

thoughtful

successful

wasteful

wonderful

skillful

plentiful

government

amusement

predicament

excitement

punishment

arrangement

fearless

careless

worthless

thoughtless

useless

reckless

_____
bonus word

_____
bonus word

shoes

sure

sugar

musician

patience

mission

occasion

physician

tension

conclusion

constitution

caution

constellation

addition

fiction

position

official

glacier

_____
bonus word

_____
bonus word

wrestle

wrong

answer

dough

unknown

knapsack

honor

listen

climb

half

island

talking

design

scratch

tonight

limb

knot

whistle

_____
bonus word

_____
bonus word

cut

cut

Week 25	Week 26	Week 27
rewrite	paragraph	imperfect
reappear	trophy	impolite
recall	nephew	impatient
recover	enough	improper
rebuild	cough	inactive
dishonest	fourth	inconvenient
disagree	Friday	incorrect
disappear	physical	inconsiderate
disappoint	roughest	preview
disconnect	pharmacy	prejudice
disapprove	fragile	prevent
misbehave	fluid	prefix
misfortune	briefly	prehistoric
misunderstand	festival	unable
misspell	stuffed	uncertain
misuse	triumph	uncomfortable
illegal	telephone	unaware
illegible	few	ungrateful

cut

cut

_____
bonus word

_____
bonus word

_____
bonus word

_____
bonus word

_____
bonus word

_____
bonus word

geology	destruct	multiply
geometry	destruction	temperature
geography	describe	vertical
geologist	description	equation
action	decorate	currency
enact	decoration	amphibian
transport	divide	intersection
import	division	environment
portable	administer	agriculture
bicycle	administration	frequency
cyclone	populate	civilization
encyclopedia	population	manufacture
autograph	infect	characteristic
automobile	infection	atmosphere
automatic	punctuate	representative
autobiography	punctuation	semicircle
telegraph	attend	substitute
photograph	attention	technology

cut

cut

_____
bonus word

_____
bonus word

_____
bonus word

_____
bonus word

_____
bonus word

_____
bonus word

Spelling List

This Week's Focus:
- Spell words with the short **u** sound
- Review other short vowel sounds
- Spell two-syllable words

STEP 1 Read and Spell	STEP 2 Copy and Spell	STEP 3 Cover and Spell

fold

1. rough

2. grudge

3. stunt

4. thumb

5. once

6. another

7. does

8. trouble

9. cousin

10. began

11. oxygen

12. copy

13. very

14. until

15. umpire

16. sudden

17. which

18. city

19. _____
   bonus word

20. _____
   bonus word

Word Meaning

Fill in the blanks with spelling words.

1. The diver used an _____ tank _____ he

   reached the surface of the water.

2. My _____ had a _____ against the _____

   who called him out.

3. Which _____ did you hurt trying to do that _____?

4. They are moving to _____ _____ next week.

5. All of a _____ it _____ to rain and I got

   _____ wet.

6. If you _____ his homework you'll get in _____.

7. I did not know _____ road to take.

My Spelling Dictation

Write the sentences. Circle the spelling words.

1. _____

   _____

2. _____

   _____

Word Study

List the spelling words that have the sound of short **u**.
Then circle the letters that make the short **u** sound.

_____ r(ou)gh _____   _____   _____

_____   _____   _____

_____   _____   _____

_____   _____   _____

Mark all of the short vowels in these words.

1. begăn   5. umpire

2. opposite   6. which

3. another   7. city

4. copy   8. until

Match syllables to make words. Write the complete word on the line.

1. trou   til   1. _____ trouble _____

2. cou   gan   2. _____

3. be   ble   3. _____

4. cop   y   4. _____

5. un   den   5. _____

6. um   sin   6. _____

7. sud   y   7. _____

8. cit   pire   8. _____

Edit for Spelling

Circle the word in each row that is spelled correctly.

1.	gruje	grudge	grudje
2.	anuther	unother	another
3.	does	duz	doez
4.	truble	drouble	trouble
5.	cuzin	cousin	cuosin
6.	oxigun	oxegun	oxygen
7.	empare	umpire	umpyre
8.	sity	citty	city
9.	entil	untill	until
10.	which	wich	whitch
11.	thum	thumb	tumb
12.	very	wery	verie

Circle the misspelled words in the sentences. Write them correctly on the lines.

1. His cuzin lives in unother sity.

   _____   _____   _____

2. The doctor gave the man oxigin entil he begun to breathe on his own.

   _____   _____   _____

3. Wunce I got into truble for doing a silly stunts.

   _____   _____   _____

4. Duz a snake have verie ruff scales on its body?

   _____   _____   _____

Building Spelling Skills

Spelling List

This Week's Focus:
- Spell words with the long **a** sound
- Identify words with open syllables

STEP 1 Read and Spell	STEP 2 Copy and Spell	STEP 3 Cover and Spell

fold

1. afraid
2. explain
3. payment
4. sleigh
5. laid
6. raise
7. straight
8. freight
9. height
10. they
11. favorite
12. April
13. able
14. radio
15. station
16. relation
17. daybreak
18. trace
19. _____
    bonus word
20. _____
    bonus word

Word Meaning

Complete the crossword puzzle using spelling words.

Across

1. a device for sending and receiving sounds through the air without using wires
5. an amount that is paid
7. a connection between two or more things
8. a carriage mounted on runners to use on snow or ice
10. frightened
11. goods carried by a truck, train, ship, or plane
13. a regular stopping place for a bus or train
14. dawn
16. put down

Down

2. the fourth month of the year
3. the thing liked best
4. not crooked
6. to tell the reason; to tell how to do something
7. to lift up
9. how tall someone is
12. to follow marks, tracks, or signs left behind
15. having the ability to do something

My Spelling Dictation

Write the sentences. Circle the spelling words.

1. _____

_____

2. _____

_____

Word Study

Fill in the missing letters to make spelling words.

> a   ai   ey   ay   aigh   ea   eigh

1. p_____ment

2. r_____se

3. th_____

4. _____ble

5. rel_____tion

6. afr_____d

7. sl_____

8. str_____t

9. f_____vorite

10. r_____dio

11. d_____br_____k

12. expl_____n

13. l_____d

14. _____pril

15. tr_____ce

16. fr_____t

17. st_____tion

18. h_____t

Count the syllables in each word.
Write the number on the line.

1. afraid ___2___

2. explain _____

3. April _____

4. able _____

5. raise _____

6. freight _____

7. they _____

8. radio _____

9. sleigh _____

10. station _____

11. payment _____

12. straight _____

13. daybreak _____

14. laid _____

15. relation _____

16. trace _____

17. favorite _____

18. height _____

Edit for Spelling

Circle the word in each row that is spelled correctly.

1. paymunt   payment   paiment
2. hight   hite   height
3. ufraid   afrayd   afraid
4. relation   relaytion   relashun
5. daybrake   daybreak   daibreak
6. layed   laed   laid
7. favorite   faverite   favorute
8. Aprul   April   april
9. radio   raddio   raideo
10. explayn   explane   explain
11. straight   strate   streat
12. rayse   raise   raize

Circle the misspelled words in the sentences. Write them correctly on the lines.

1. Aprul is my faverute month of the year.

   _____ _____

2. We made the last paiment on our new slay.

   _____ _____

3. Can you explane how a radeo works?

   _____ _____

4. The workmen layed a straite track for the frayt train.

   _____ _____ _____

Spelling List

This Week's Focus:
- Spell words with the long **e** sound
- Spell words with the long **u** sound
- Recognize the short vowel sound in **been**

STEP 1 Read and Spell

fold

STEP 2 Copy and Spell

STEP 3 Cover and Spell

1. fifteen
2. referee
3. eager
4. easily
5. ready
6. please
7. ecology
8. maybe
9. been
10. only
11. universe
12. future
13. communicate
14. beautiful
15. unusual
16. cute
17. cube
18. fuel
19. _____
   bonus word
20. _____
   bonus word

Word Meaning

Fill in the blanks with spelling words.

1. Number _____ was _____ to hear

   the _____'s decision.

2. _____ put that wooden _____ with

   the _____ design on the table.

3. Is the spaceship filled with _____ so it is _____

   to explore the _____?

4. That is _____ the most _____ painting in the museum.

5. Was the speaker able to _____ how important the study

   of _____ is to the _____ of our world?

6. _____ three people have _____ chosen to perform today.

My Spelling Dictation

Write the sentences. Circle the spelling words.

1. _____

   _____

2. _____

   _____

Word Study

Write the spelling words in the correct boxes.

cube	fifteen	eager	universe	referee	future
easily	ready	please	beautiful	maybe	only
cute	ecology	unusual	communicate	fuel	

words with the sound of long **e**	words with the sound of long **u**

Count the syllables in each word. Write the number on the line.

1. referee _____

2. universe _____

3. maybe _____

4. ecology _____

5. been _____

6. communicate _____

7. eager _____

8. beautiful _____

9. unusual _____

10. cube _____

11. easily _____

12. only _____

13. fifteen _____

14. ready _____

Edit for Spelling

Circle the word in each row that is spelled correctly.

1. eeger	eager	eagar
2. ready	reedy	reade
3. cute	kute	qute
4. binn	been	bene
5. please	pleaze	pleese
6. butifull	beautuful	beautiful
7. feul	fewl	fuel
8. easily	eesily	eazuly
9. fuchur	fewture	future
10. maybee	maybe	maibee
11. fiftene	fiteen	fifteen
12. coob	cube	kube

Circle the misspelled words in the sentences. Write them correctly on the lines.

1. Plez have the fiftene hats reddy by 5:00 p.m.

   _____   _____   _____

2. The refree must comunikate using ownlee signs.

   _____   _____   _____

3. She was eegir to buy that unuzual stone kube.

   _____   _____   _____

4. Father has bin to the gas station to add fewl to the car for our trip.

   _____   _____

This Week's Focus:
- Spell words with the long **o** sound
- Spell words in the present and past tenses

STEP 1 Read and Spell

STEP 2 Copy and Spell

STEP 3 Cover and Spell

fold

1. obey
2. ocean
3. poem
4. echo
5. hello
6. wrote
7. goal
8. approach
9. owner
10. tomorrow
11. program
12. broken
13. potato
14. throat
15. oldest
16. followed
17. spoken
18. awoke
19. _____ bonus word
20. _____ bonus word

Word Meaning

Complete these tasks using spelling words.

1. Write words that rhyme with these words.

    a. wrote _____   c. stole _____

    b. boldest _____   d. loner _____

2. Match each word to its meaning.

    a. tomorrow   _____ a form of writing that may rhyme

    b. poem   _____ one who owns something

    c. ocean   _____ the day after today

    d. goal   _____ a listing of what will be performed

    e. program   _____ a great body of salt water

    f. owner   _____ a repeated sound made by reflected sound waves

    g. echo   _____ a result which someone works toward

3. Write the spelling words that are the opposites of these words.

    a. disobey _____   d. slept _____

    b. good-bye _____   e. led _____

    c. leave _____   f. repaired _____

My Spelling Dictation

Write the sentences. Circle the spelling words.

1. _____

   _____

2. _____

   _____

Word Study

Circle the letter or letters that make the long **o** sound.

1. o b e y
2. g o a l
3. p r o g r a m
4. t h r o a t
5. p o e m
6. o c e a n
7. t o m o r r o w
8. o l d e s t
9. h e l l o
10. a p p r o a c h
11. b r o k e n
12. s p o k e n
13. w r o t e
14. o w n e r
15. p o t a t o
16. a w o k e

Circle the correct word or words to show if the verb is present or past tense.

1. wrote   **present**   **past**
2. broken   **present**   **past**
3. obey   **present**   **past**
4. awoke   **present**   **past**
5. followed   **present**   **past**
6. spoken   **present**   **past**
7. approach   **present**   **past**
8. obeyed   **present**   **past**
9. write   **present**   **past**
10. approached   **present**   **past**
11. break   **present**   **past**
12. speak   **present**   **past**

Write the past tense form of each verb.

1. follow _____
2. write _____
3. break _____
4. awake _____

Edit for Spelling

Circle the word in each row that is spelled correctly.

1. obay	obey	odey
2. ocean	ochun	osean
3. pome	poam	poem
4. ownar	owner	ownr
5. approach	uproch	upproach
6. rote	wroat	wrote
7. gole	goal	goel
8. putato	patato	potato
9. tomorro	tomarrow	tomorrow
10. program	progrum	porgram
11. troat	throat	throte
12. awoak	awuke	awoke

Circle the misspelled words in the sentences. Write them correctly on the lines.

1. The sailor's gole is to set sail on the oshun tomorro.

   _____ _____ _____

2. Did the oldist boy obay the rules?

   _____ _____

3. The borken piece of putato was stuck in his throte.

   _____ _____ _____

4. The dog's onner rote a pome about his pet.

   _____ _____

Spelling List

This Week's Focus:
- Spell contractions
- Learn the homophones **who's** and **whose**

STEP 1 Read and Spell	**STEP 2** Copy and Spell	**STEP 3** Cover and Spell

fold

1. I'll
2. they've
3. don't
4. we're
5. didn't
6. isn't
7. couldn't
8. haven't
9. o'clock
10. you're
11. who's
12. whose
13. aren't
14. it's
15. doesn't
16. there's
17. won't
18. I've
19. _____ bonus word
20. _____ bonus word

Word Meaning

Fill in the blanks using spelling words.

1. I think _____ too late for us to go now.

2. He _____ find his homework, and he _____ have time
   to look for it.

3. We _____ have enough money for tickets so we _____
   going to the ballgame.

4. _____ coming to meet the three _____ train?

Write the long form of these contractions.

1. they've _____

2. we're _____

3. you're _____

4. I've _____

5. isn't _____

6. haven't _____

7. doesn't _____

8. there's _____

My Spelling Dictation

Write the sentences. Circle the spelling words.

1. _____

   _____

2. _____

   _____

Word Study

Write the contraction and the missing letters.

	Contraction	Missing letters
1. I will	I'll	w i
2. have not		
3. we are		
4. they have		
5. could not		
6. you are		
7. there is		
8. does not		
9. it is		
10. I have		
11. who is		
12. do not		

Write contractions for these words.

1. they are	_____		5. was not	_____
2. we will	_____		6. they will	_____
3. would not	_____		7. has not	_____
4. she is	_____		8. he is	_____

Which two spelling words are homophones? _____ _____

Edit for Spelling

Write the missing apostrophe in the correct place.

1. Ill

2. wont

3. oclock

4. doesnt

5. theres

6. its

7. didnt

8. arent

9. youre

10. havent

11. theyve

12. dont

13. were

14. isnt

15. couldnt

Circle the misspelled words in the sentences. Write them correctly on the lines.

1. Culdn't you fix the broken bike?

   _____

2. Who's coat is that?

   _____

3. Ive' got to be there by 6 oclock.

   _____   _____

4. Theyv'e traveled to Florida but did'nt have time to visit us.

   _____   _____

5. Were going skating. Wo'nt you come with us?

   _____   _____

6. Ill try to find out whose going to sing.

   _____   _____

WEEK 6

Spelling List

This Week's Focus:
- Spell words with the long **i** sound
- Add the ending **-ing**

STEP 1 Read and Spell	STEP 2 Copy and Spell	STEP 3 Cover and Spell

fold

1. idea
2. silent
3. myself
4. lying
5. apply
6. knight
7. quite
8. I'm
9. license
10. buy
11. inquire
12. higher
13. variety
14. smiling
15. diagram
16. rhyme
17. widest
18. python
19. _____
   bonus word
20. _____
   bonus word

Word Meaning

Complete the crossword puzzle using spelling words.

Down

1. making no sound
4. to ask for information
5. completely; very
7. at a greater height
8. a number of different types of things
10. making a false statement

Across

2. wearing a happy facial expression
3. an official permit
6. a mounted soldier in the Middle Ages
9. a thought
11. what poems often do
12. broadest from side to side
13. a drawing or plan that makes something clearer
14. a type of large snake

My Spelling Dictation

Write the sentences. Circle the spelling words.

1. _____

   _____

2. _____

   _____

Word Study

Circle the letter or letters that make the long **i** sound.

1. lying	5. widest	9. diagram	13. variety	17. license
2. idea	6. rhyme	10. smiling	14. I'm	18. inquire
3. silent	7. myself	11. knight	15. buy	
4. python	8. apply	12. quite	16. higher	

Fill in the blank with the correct form of the word in parentheses.

1. Was he _____ or telling the truth?
   (lie)

2. Anna was _____ as she opened the present.
   (smile)

3. The police officer will _____ if anyone saw the accident.
   (inquire)

4. Who will _____ you those new shoes?
   (buy)

5. I should _____ for the new job.
   (apply)

6. Grace can climb _____ than you can.
   (high)

7. Which ribbon is the _____?
   (wide)

42

Edit for Spelling

Circle the words that are spelled correctly.

sylent	python	hier	upply
rhyme	inqire	widist	diagram
kwite	lisence	myself	smilling
bi	lying	idea	knite

Circle the misspelled words in the sentences.
Write them correctly on the lines.

1. The knite made a diagarm of the castle's defenses.

   _____ _____

2. I found miself smileng at the silunt movie.

   _____ _____ _____

3. A pyton crawled hier up into the tree.

   _____ _____

4. He is not quit finished with the rime.

   _____ _____

5. Im going to bye some of each varitee of candy for the party.

   _____ _____ _____

Spelling List

This Week's Focus:
- Spell words with the /oo/ sound spelled **oo**, **ou**, **ue**, **u**, and **ew**
- Spell words with the vowel sound in **look**

STEP 1 Read and Spell

STEP 2 Copy and Spell

STEP 3 Cover and Spell

fold

1. gloomy
2. school
3. choose
4. loose
5. route
6. clue
7. truth
8. duty
9. ruin
10. Tuesday
11. usually
12. threw
13. understood
14. neighborhood
15. rookie
16. could
17. should
18. bulletin
19. _____
   bonus word
20. _____
   bonus word

Word Meaning

Answer these questions using spelling words.

1. Which spelling words rhyme with these words?

   a. would _____

   b. spool _____

   c. flew _____

   d. beauty _____

   e. cookie _____

   f. booth _____

2. Which spelling words have about the same meanings as these words?

   a. dreary _____

   b. tossed _____

   c. beginner _____

   d. destroy _____

   e. pathway _____

   f. baggy _____

   g. select _____

   h. hint _____

   i. honesty _____

   j. announcement _____

   k. comprehended _____

   l. regularly _____

My Spelling Dictation

Write the sentences. Circle the spelling words.

1. _____

   _____

2. _____

   _____

Word Study

Write the spelling words in the correct boxes.

gloomy	should	clue	choose	understood	duty
rookie	route	ruin	neighborhood	usually	threw
school	Tuesday	bulletin	loose	truth	could

vowel sound in **look**	vowel sound in **too**
rookie	

Match the syllables to make words.
Write the complete words on the lines.

1. gloom   ie   1. _____

2. rook   in   2. _____

3. du   y   3. _____

4. ru   day   4. _____

5. Tues   ty   5. _____

Edit for Spelling

Circle the words that are spelled correctly.

gloomee	klue	chosse	upply
school	truth	dooty	usually
rute	Teusday	bulletin	ruin
rookie	throo	shud	culd

Circle the misspelled words in the sentences.
Write them correctly on the lines.

1. Will the gloome weather rooin our picnic?

   _____   _____

2. I need a klew to who is telling the trooth.

   _____   _____

3. The kids in my nayberhood usully play after skool.

   _____   _____   _____

4. He thru the ball to the ruky.

   _____   _____

5. He undrestood the news bulliten on Tusday.

   _____   _____   _____

Spelling List

This Week's Focus:
- Spell words with the diphthongs **oi** and **oy**
- Spell words with the digraphs **ou** and **ow**

STEP 1 Read and Spell	**STEP 2** Copy and Spell	**STEP 3** Cover and Spell

1. spoil
2. choice
3. avoid
4. moisture
5. oyster
6. royal
7. employ
8. annoy
9. ground
10. house
11. sprout
12. mountain
13. allow
14. ourselves
15. somehow
16. ounce
17. amount
18. boundary
19. _____ bonus word
20. _____ bonus word

Fill in the blanks with spelling words.

1. _____ on the _____ trail made it too wet to climb.

2. The raw _____ will _____ if it's not kept cold.

3. Is one _____ of sugar the correct _____ for this recipe?

4. Don't _____ your dogs to _____ the neighbor's cat.

5. Do you think the _____ family would _____ me as a palace guard?

6. A plant began to _____ along the _____ between my yard and the _____ next door.

7. I will _____ stepping on the wet _____ in my new shoes.

8. We all make the _____ to take care of _____.

My Spelling Dictation

Write the sentences. Circle the spelling words.

1. _____

_____

2. _____

_____

Fill in the missing letters to make spelling words.

oi   oy

1. ch_____ce

2. r_____al

3. sp_____l

4. av_____d

5. empl_____

6. m_____sture

7. _____ster

8. ann_____

ou   ow

9. gr_____nd

10. h_____se

11. b_____ndary

12. all_____

13. m_____ntain

14. _____rselves

15. someh_____

16. _____nce

Divide these words into syllables.

1. avoid   _____

2. oyster   _____

3. royal   _____

4. employ   _____

5. annoy   _____

6. mountain   _____

7. ourselves _____

8. allow   _____

9. somehow   _____

10. amount   _____

Edit for Spelling

Circle the word in each row that is spelled correctly.

1. spoyl   spoil   spoll

2. royul   royle   royal

3. avode   uvoid   avoid

4. oister   oyster   oystre

5. ounce   ownce   oince

6. amont   amount   umount

7. sumhow   somehou   somehow

8. areselfs   ourselves   ourselfs

9. annoy   unnoy   anoye

10. boundery   boundary   boundry

Circle the misspelled words in the sentences. Write them correctly on the lines.

1. Mr. and Mrs. Ruiz enploy a maid to clean their howse.

   _____   _____

2. It was his choyse to climb to the top of the mountin.

   _____   _____

3. The morning dew left moysture on the grownd.

   _____   _____

4. Sumhow one ownce doesn't seem to be the correct umount.

   _____   _____   _____   _____

Spelling List

This Week's Focus:
- Spell the three types of compound words (one word, two words, and hyphenated words)

STEP 1 Read and Spell	STEP 2 Copy and Spell	STEP 3 Cover and Spell

1. baby-sit
2. first aid
3. flashlight
4. high school
5. goalkeeper
6. all right
7. airmail
8. one-way
9. bodyguard
10. something
11. good-bye
12. birthday
13. outside
14. everybody
15. everyone
16. anything
17. themselves
18. himself
19. _____ bonus word
20. _____ bonus word

fold

52

Word Meaning

Complete these tasks using spelling words.

1. There are three ways a compound word can be formed.
   Write a spelling word for each way.

   a. hyphenated _____

   b. two words _____

   c. one word _____

2. Which spelling words refer to people?

   _____ _____ _____

   _____ _____ _____

3. What would someone give you if you were injured? _____

4. Which words stand for "all people"?

   _____ _____

5. Which spelling words mean the opposite of these words?

   a. hello _____   c. inside _____

   b. nothing _____   d. nobody _____

My Spelling Dictation

Write the sentences. Circle the spelling words.

1. _____

_____

2. _____

_____

Word Study

Use one word from each box to make compound words.
Cross out each word as you use it.
Check the spelling list to make sure that you form the compound words correctly.

out	thing
birth	bye
high	self
good	mail
him	right
some	day
all	school
air	side

_____

_____

_____

_____

_____

_____

_____

_____

Circle the letter or letters that make the long vowel sounds in the words below.
Then circle the sound that the letter or letters make. Some words will have two long vowels circled.

1. first aid   (a)   e   i   o   u

2. flashlight   a   e   i   o   u

3. one-way   a   e   i   o   u

4. everyone   a   e   i   o   u

5. maybe   a   e   i   o   u

6. anything   a   e   i   o   u

7. baby-sit   a   e   i   o   u

Edit for Spelling

Circle the word in each row that is spelled correctly.

1.	baby sit	babysit	baby-sit
2.	first aid	firstaid	first-aid
3.	flash light	flashlight	flash-light
4.	all right	allright	all-right
5.	air mail	airmail	air-mail
6.	one way	oneway	one-way
7.	birth day	birthday	birth-day
8.	good bye	goodbey	good-bye
9.	any thing	anything	any-thing
10.	high school	highschool	high-school

Circle the misspelled words in the sentences. Write them correctly on the lines.

1. The coach gave first-ade to the injured goal keeper.

   _____   _____

2. Is it allright to send the birth day card by air-mail?

   _____   _____   _____

3. The bodygard used a flashlite to find his way in the dark.

   _____   _____

4. Evrybody is playing out side on the lawn.

   _____   _____

This Week's Focus:
- Spell words with the /**aw**/ sound

STEP **1** Read and Spell	STEP **2** Copy and Spell	STEP **3** Cover and Spell

fold

1. stalk
2. off
3. because
4. brought
5. called
6. drawn
7. awful
8. awkward
9. lawyer
10. daughter
11. fault
12. author
13. always
14. already
15. although
16. belong
17. office
18. haul
19. _____ bonus word
20. _____ bonus word

Word Meaning

Fill in the blanks with spelling words.

1. The _____ felt _____ when she spilled her mother's lunch on the floor.

2. Has the _____ of the book _____ the illustrations also?

3. The _____ was _____ in her _____ by 7 o'clock this morning.

4. Grandmother _____ _____ presents when she came to visit us.

5. The picnic was _____ off _____ of the rainstorm.

6. It is my _____ the vase fell _____ the table.

7. The _____ young calf pulled the corn from the _____.

My Spelling Dictation

Write the sentences. Circle the spelling words.

1. _____

_____

2. _____

_____

Word Study

Circle the letter or letters that have the same vowel sound you hear in **ball**.

1. stalk

2. off

3. because

4. brought

5. called

6. drawn

7. haul

8. belong

9. office

10. although

11. awkward

12. already

13. daughter

14. lawyer

15. author

Write the spelling words that are synonyms for these words.

1. terrible _____

2. clumsy _____

3. mistake _____

4. writer _____

5. forever _____

6. be suitable _____

7. carry _____

8. away _____

Complete the sentences using the synonyms from above.

1. The _____ dancer had an _____ fall.
   (clumsy)   (terrible)

2. My favorite _____'s work will be remembered _____.
   (writer)   (forever)

3. Did you _____ the junk _____ to the dump?
   (carry)   (away)

Edit for Spelling

Circle the 11 misspelled words below.
Write them correctly on the lines.

The Awful Accident

Mrs. Bernard, the lawyre, colled home to say she wouldn't be home for dinner becawse she had work to do. She asked her dotter to bring her something to eat at the ofice.

Alice brote her mother some soup and salad. While she was pouring the soup, the awkword girl spilled it all over the papers on her mother's desk.

Alice felt awfull. She knew her mother had draun up the papers for a client who was coming to sign them in the morning.

Her mother said, "It's your fawlt the papers are ruined, but I know it was an accident. Don't worry. I all ways save a copy of important papers on my computer. I will print out a new set after dinner. Now let's clean up this mess and eat."

_____   _____   _____

_____   _____   _____

_____   _____   _____

_____   _____

Building Spelling Skills

Spelling List

This Week's Focus:
- Spell words with the endings **-ed**, **-ing**, **-er**, and **-est**

STEP 1 Read and Spell	STEP 2 Copy and Spell	STEP 3 Cover and Spell
1. surrounded		
2. skiing		
3. swimming		
4. loving		
5. studied		
6. traveling		
7. carried		
8. trading		
9. bragged		
10. worried		
11. beginning		
12. exciting		
13. finished		
14. laughed		
15. quickest		
16. weaker		
17. tiniest		
18. lonelier		
19. _____ bonus word		
20. _____ bonus word		

fold

Word Meaning

Complete these tasks using spelling words.

1. Write the verbs that are in the past tense.

   _____   _____   _____

   _____   _____

   _____   _____

2. Which words name activities you can do outdoors?

   _____   _____

3. Write the word that means…

   a. completed a task   _____

   b. going from one place to another   _____

   c. not as strong as someone else   _____

   d. concerned about something   _____

   e. the fastest one   _____

   f. made a happy sound   _____

   g. talked about how good you are   _____

   h. the smallest one   _____

My Spelling Dictation

Write the sentences. Circle the spelling words.

1. _____

   _____

2. _____

   _____

Word Study

Add **ing** to the base word. Write the new word on the line.
Check the box that tells how you changed the word.

		no change	drop **e**	double final consonant
1.	laugh ___laughing___	✔		
2.	love _____			
3.	begin _____			
4.	ski _____			
5.	swim _____			

Add **ed** to the base word. Check the box that tells how you changed the word.

		no change	change **y** to **i**	drop **e**
1.	surround _____			
2.	study _____			
3.	trade _____			
4.	carry _____			
5.	excite _____			

Add **er** or **est** to each verb to make a comparison.

1. A cheetah is the _____ member of the cat family.
   (quick)

2. I was _____ than my roommate at camp.
   (lonely)

3. Matthew was _____ than his friend in nursery school.
   (weak)

4. A hummingbird is the _____ bird.
   (tiny)

     62

Edit for Spelling

Circle the word in each row that is spelled correctly.

1. loveing   loving   luving

2. lonelir   lonlier   lonelier

3. surounded   surrounded   surounddded

4. trading   tradeing   tradding

Circle the 9 misspelled words below.
Write them correctly on the lines.

The Bragging Skier

George braged about how great he was at sking. He laffed at the other skiers at the begining of the downhill race. He was sure he would win.

It was exsiting swooping down the slopes. Halfway through the race, George became worred. Although he was travling as fast as he could, he was not the qwickest racer.

George was very upset when he finish last. "I'll never brag before a race again!" he cried.

_____   _____   _____

_____   _____   _____

_____   _____   _____

Spelling List

This Week's Focus:
- Spell plural forms of words by adding endings to base words
- Spell words with irregular plural forms

STEP 1 Read and Spell

STEP 2 Copy and Spell

STEP 3 Cover and Spell

fold

1. countries

2. addresses

3. women

4. lessons

5. people

6. skis

7. friends

8. roofs

9. calves

10. fences

11. flies

12. lives

13. cherries

14. businesses

15. guesses

16. families

17. leaves

18. pictures

19. _____
   bonus word

20. _____
   bonus word

Word Meaning

Complete the crossword puzzle using spelling words.

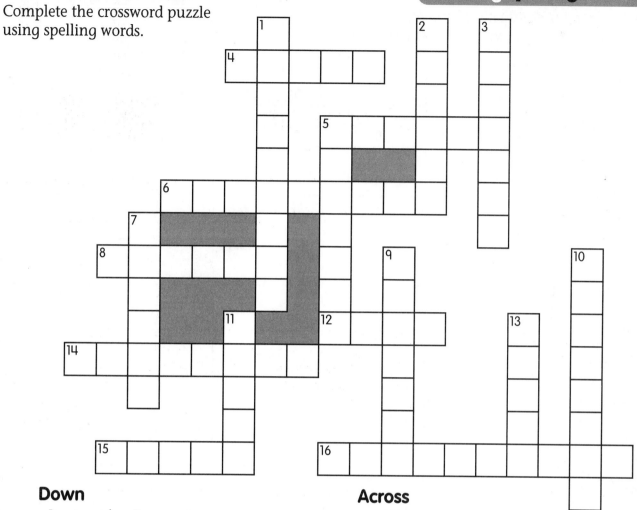

Down

1. several nations
2. more than one baby cow
3. opinions formed without exact knowledge
5. things to be learned
7. railings or walls around yards
9. people who know and like each other
10. groups of relatives
11. more than one life
13. coverings over buildings

Across

4. more than one adult female
5. the parts of a tree that make its food
6. places where mail is directed
8. more than one person
12. two long runners used to go down snowy hills
14. sweet round fruits
15. small flying insects
16. commercial activities

My Spelling Dictation

Write the sentences. Circle the spelling words.

1. _____

_____

2. _____

_____

Word Study

Change each singular noun to its plural form.
Check the box that tells how you changed the word.

	add **s** or **es**	drop **e** and add **s**	change **y** to **i** and add **es**	change **f** to **v** and add **es**
1. ski _____skis_____	✔			
2. country _____				
3. fence _____				
4. leaf _____				
5. roof _____				
6. fly _____				
7. life _____				
8. family _____				
9. guess _____				
10. picture _____				
11. calf _____				
12. lesson _____				
13. business _____				
14. friend _____				
15. cherry _____				
16. address _____				

Write the plural forms of these nouns.

woman _____   person _____

Edit for Spelling

Circle the words that are spelled correctly.

countrys	addresses	womun	lessons
peeple	skiis	friends	cherrys
leaves	rooves	calfs	fences
flys	families	lifes	businesses
freinds	pitures	roofs	gesses

Circle the misspelled words in the sentences.
Write them correctly on the lines.

1. The two womun taught swimming lessuns to many peopel.

   _____   _____   _____

2. I have the adresses of many frends living in countrys around the world.

   _____   _____   _____

3. One of Mr. Lewis's busnesses is taking pitchers of familees.

   _____   _____   _____

4. His calfs became ill after eating green cherrys.

   _____   _____

Spelling List

This Week's Focus:
- Spell words with the /ər/ sound
- Spell two- and three-syllable words

STEP 1 Read and Spell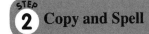

fold

1. urgent
2. Thursday
3. purpose
4. thirsty
5. camera
6. wonder
7. smuggler
8. remember
9. surprise
10. earth
11. certain
12. person
13. dollar
14. color
15. collar
16. early
17. mayor
18. doctor
19. _____
    bonus word
20. _____
    bonus word

STEP 2 Copy and Spell

STEP 3 Cover and Spell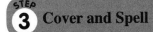

Word Meaning

Complete the crossword puzzle using spelling words.
There is one word <u>not</u> on the spelling list. See if you can figure it out.

Across

1. needing a drink of water
3. a reason for doing something
6. a person who brings things into the country illegally
7. a person who heads a city or town government
8. a human being
10. ground; dirt
11. a piece of money worth 100 cents
12. an instrument used to take photographs
13. the part of a shirt that is around the neck
14. red, yellow, blue, etc.
15. to be curious about something

Down

2. something unexpected
4. the opposite of **forget**
5. the day after Wednesday
9. to be sure about something
11. a healer of sick people
13. the opposite of **hot**

My Spelling Dictation

Write the sentences. Circle the spelling words.

1. _____

   _____

2. _____

   _____

Circle the letters that make the /ər/ sound.

1. ⊙ur⊙gent
2. thirsty
3. collar
4. camera
5. wonder
6. doctor

7. Thursday
8. earth
9. certain
10. color
11. purpose
12. mayor

13. smuggler
14. surprise
15. person
16. dollar
17. early

Match syllables to make spelling words.
Write the complete words on the lines.

1. ur	y	1. _____
2. thirst	gler	2. _____
3. won	gent	3. _____
4. smug	ly	4. _____
5. pur	tain	5. _____
6. col	der	6. _____
7. cer	pose	7. _____
8. may	prise	8. _____
9. ear	lar	9. _____
10. sur	or	10. _____

Edit for Spelling

Correct the spelling of the /ər/ sound in these words.

ar   or   ur   er   ear

1. irgent _____

2. camira _____

3. irth _____

4. dollir _____

5. wondir _____

6. mayir _____

7. pirson _____

8. doctir _____

9. irly _____

10. colir _____

Circle the misspelled words in the sentences. Write them correctly on the lines.

1. The mayir gave a speech erly Thirsday morning.

_____ _____ _____

2. It's irgent that the thirstee man gets water quickly.

_____ _____

3. I'm cirtain the docter can help me.

_____ _____

4. Did that persun remember the perpose of our meeting?

_____ _____ _____

5. A smugglar tried to sell a stolen kamera for one doller.

_____ _____

Spelling List

This Week's Focus:
• Spell words with **r**-controlled vowel sounds

STEP 1 Read and Spell	STEP 2 Copy and Spell	STEP 3 Cover and Spell

fold

1. square

2. stare

3. dairy

4. area

5. January

6. dictionary

7. daring

8. beware

9. argument

10. large

11. partner

12. guarding

13. article

14. orchestra

15. ordinary

16. important

17. force

18. before

19. _____
   bonus word

20. _____
   bonus word

Word Meaning

Answer the questions using spelling words.

1. What would you use to look up the meaning of a word? _____

2. Where is milk put into bottles or cartons? _____

3. What do you call...?

    a. a large group of musicians playing together _____

    b. a person you team up with _____

4. Which spelling word means...?

    a. be careful _____   d. protecting _____

    b. brave _____   e. power _____

    c. disagreement _____

5. Which spelling word is an antonym for...?

    a. small _____   c. unique _____

    b. after _____

6. Which spelling word rhymes with...?

    a. stare _____   d. barge _____

    b. wearing _____   e. horse _____

    c. declare _____   f. adore _____

My Spelling Dictation

Write the sentences. Circle the spelling words.

1. _____

_____

2. _____

_____

Word Study

Write the spelling words in the correct boxes.

square	argument	orchestra	dairy	stare	large
force	important	area	partner	guarding	ordinary
January	article	dictionary	daring	before	beware

words with the sound of **a** in **fair**	words with the sound of **ar** in **car**	words with the sound of **or** in **store**

Fill in the missing letters.

1. argu_____

2. be_____

3. _____ner

4. or_____tra

5. im_____tant

6. dic_____ary

7. ar_____cle

8. _____fore

9. ordi_____y

10. dar_____

Edit for Spelling

Circle the words that are spelled correctly.

kware	stare	derry
partner	bewear	article
larje	forse	orchestra
befor	area	Januery
dicshunary	garding	argument
daring	ordinery	importent

Circle the misspelled words in the sentences.
Write them correctly on the lines.

1. Members of the police fource were garding the orkestra conductor.

   _____ _____ _____

2. An inportant artikle was in the newspaper last Jenuary.

   _____ _____ _____

3. Bewair of argumints with lawrge strangers.

   _____ _____ _____

4. That green areeu is called the town sqware.

   _____ _____

Spelling List

This Week's Focus:
- Spell words with the schwa sound
- Spell two-syllable words
- Review the /ər/ sound

STEP 1 Read and Spell

STEP 2 Copy and Spell

STEP 3 Cover and Spell

fold

1. about
2. algebra
3. quiet
4. other
5. compare
6. thousand
7. happen
8. different
9. along
10. equator
11. dozen
12. animal
13. second
14. region
15. quarter
16. lecture
17. puncture
18. again
19. _____
   bonus word
20. _____
   bonus word

Word Meaning

Fill in the blanks with spelling words.

1. The climate along the _____ is very _____ from the
   climate in Alaska.

2. Will you _____ this book to the _____ book?

3. I am taking _____ as my math class next year.

4. Do you know what will _____ if you do that _____?

5. Please fix the _____ in my bike's tire.

6. I go to the river when I need peace and _____.

7. The _____ at the library costs only a _____.

8. I came in _____ place among one _____ people!

9. My favorite _____ is the zebra.

My Spelling Dictation

Write the sentences. Circle the spelling words.

1. _____

   _____

2. _____

   _____

Word Study

Write the symbol ə over the letter or letters that make the schwa sound.

ə
about

algebra	other	dozen	region
thousand	happen	animal	again
along	quiet	second	puncture

Divide these words into syllables.

1. about _____

2. other _____

3. compare _____

4. happen _____

5. along _____

6. region _____

7. quarter _____

8. second _____

9. lecture _____

10. puncture _____

11. thousand _____

12. quiet _____

13. algebra _____

14. different _____

15. equator _____

16. dozen _____

17. again _____

18. animal _____

Edit for Spelling

Circle the 12 misspelled words below.
Write them correctly on the lines.

Danger Along the Equator

It was kwiet in the jungle. Tomas huddled like a scared animle

in the brush. He had come to this rejun to give a lechure ubout using

diferent rainforest plants in medicine. But now he was stranded on

a deserted, unpaved road somewhere near the equater. A tire on his

vehicle was puntured, and the vehicle was stalled on the side of the

road. Tomas had a broken leg, and it was almost dark.

What would hapen next? Only a few travelers had passed him

allong the road as he had driven toward the field hospital where he was

to have spoken. Now, if he ever made it to his destination, instead of

speaking, he would be a patient. As the secunds dragged by, Tomas

peered down the road agin and then slipped into unconsciousness.

_____   _____   _____

_____   _____   _____

_____   _____   _____

_____   _____   _____

Spelling List

This Week's Focus:
- Spell words with the consonant digraphs **wh**, **ch**, **tch**, **sh**, and **th**
- Spell plural forms of words

STEP 1 Read and Spell	**STEP 2** Copy and Spell	**STEP 3** Cover and Spell

fold

1. awhile
2. where
3. thought
4. athletes
5. truthful
6. purchases
7. exchange
8. though
9. rhythm
10. children
11. chocolates
12. friendship
13. together
14. white
15. watches
16. arithmetic
17. months
18. length
19. _____ bonus word
20. _____ bonus word

Word Meaning

Answer the questions using spelling words.

1. What is the plural form of these nouns?

    a. athlete _____

    b. watch _____

    c. child _____

    d. chocolate _____

2. Which word has both of these meanings?

    a. buys things <u>and</u> the things you buy   _____

    b. looks at something <u>and</u> timepieces worn on your wrist   _____

    c. a place where stocks are bought and sold <u>and</u> to
       trade things   _____

3. Which spelling word describes one thing dancers
   <u>and</u> musicians need?   _____

4. Which spelling words contain the digraph **th**?
   Circle every **th** that has the sound you hear in **thin** or **the**.

   _____   _____   _____

   _____   _____   _____

   _____   _____   _____

My Spelling Dictation

Write the sentences. Circle the spelling words.

1. _____

   _____

2. _____

   _____

Word Study

Fill in the missing digraphs to make spelling words.

> wh   ch   tch   sh   th

1. a_____ile

2. _____ought

3. ex_____ange

4. rhy_____m

5. _____ocolates

6. wa_____es

7. _____ere

8. a_____letes

9. tru_____ful

10. pur_____ases

11. _____ough

12. friend_____ip

13. leng_____

14. _____ite

15. _____ildren

16. ari_____metic

17. mon_____s

18. toge_____er

Write the plural form of each noun.

1. month _____

2. athlete _____

3. child _____

4. chocolate _____

5. watch _____

6. purchase _____

Using what you know about forming plural nouns, circle the irregular plural nouns below.

cities

sleighs

radios

people

potatoes

women

skis

families

Edit for Spelling

Circle the words that are spelled correctly.

athletes	rythm	together
troothful	awhile	childern
choclates	length	purchasis
though	frendship	exchange

Circle the misspelled words in the sentences.
Write them correctly on the lines.

1. Both atheletes trained for munths before the track meet.

   _____   _____

2. Did the childrn study for their arithmutic test?

   _____   _____

3. How many perchases of choclates were made on Saturday?

   _____   _____

4. Our frendship has lasted a long time even though we argue sometimes.

   _____

5. I'm going to exchanj my gold waches for wite leather boots.

   _____   _____   _____

Spelling List

This Week's Focus:
- Spell words with the variant sounds of **g** and **c**

STEP 1 Read and Spell

1. signal
2. regular
3. generous
4. energy
5. bridge
6. genius
7. dangerous
8. segment
9. figure
10. country
11. circle
12. concert
13. peaceful
14. nice
15. since
16. electric
17. dancing
18. decided
19. _____ bonus word
20. _____ bonus word

STEP 2 Copy and Spell

fold

STEP 3 Cover and Spell

Word Meaning

Complete the crossword puzzle using spelling words.

Down

1. something built over a river so people and vehicles can go across
2. the opposite of **selfish**
4. happening again and again at the same time
5. land; nation; region
6. made up your mind
7. from then until now
10. a perfectly round shape
11. a form or shape
13. a part of the whole thing
14. pleasing; agreeable

Across

3. charged with electrical energy
6. the opposite of **safe**
8. signs giving notice of something
9. free from strife; calm
12. an exceptionally intelligent or gifted person
15. the capacity for doing work
16. a musical performance

My Spelling Dictation

Write the sentences. Circle the spelling words.

1. _____

   _____

2. _____

   _____

Word Study

Circle the sounds for **g** and **c**.

	Sounds for **g**			Sounds for **c**	
1. signal	/g/	/j/	9. country	/k/	/s/
2. energy	/g/	/j/	10. peaceful	/k/	/s/
3. bridge	/g/	/j/	11. since	/k/	/s/
4. figure	/g/	/j/	12. electric	/k/	/s/
5. dangerous	/g/	/j/	13. nice	/k/	/s/
6. regular	/g/	/j/	14. decided	/k/	/s/
7. segment	/g/	/j/	15. circle	/k/	/s/
8. generous	/g/	/j/	16. concert	/k/	/s/

Divide these words into syllables.

1. country _____

2. signal _____

3. peaceful _____

4. segment _____

5. figure _____

6. circle _____

7. dancing _____

8. genius _____

9. dangerous _____

10. generous _____

11. electric _____

12. regular _____

Edit for Spelling

Circle the words that are spelled correctly.

dancing	regular	desided
jenerous	sinse	figure
cirkle	danjerous	electric
signal	country	bridje
segment	energy	nise
peacful	concert	genius

Circle the misspelled words in the sentences. Write them correctly on the lines.

1. My family goes to the cuntry because it is so pieceful there.

   _____   _____

2. It was dangirous work building a brige over that canyon.

   _____   _____

3. Mr. Ruiz has been very genrous sinse he won the lottery.

   _____   _____

4. Everyone was dansing in a cirkle at the concirt.

   _____   _____

Spelling List

This Week's Focus:
- Spell words with the final /l/ sound spelled **le**, **el**, or **al**
- Spell multisyllabic words
- Review the schwa sound

STEP 1 Read and Spell

STEP 2 Copy and Spell

STEP 3 Cover and Spell

fold

1. eagle
2. example
3. towel
4. special
5. legal
6. little
7. whole
8. several
9. terrible
10. label
11. question
12. frequent
13. telescope
14. instead
15. instrument
16. celebrate
17. declare
18. address
19. _____
   bonus word
20. _____
   bonus word

Word Meaning

Fill in the blanks with spelling words.

1. Harry had a _____ nightmare about a gigantic _____ that carried him away.

2. What musical _____ do you play?

3. Ann invited _____ friends over to help _____ her birthday.

4. _____ the _____ and place it on the package before you mail it.

5. My dad has a _____ for studying the stars and planets.

6. Did they eat the _____ cake or only a _____ piece?

7. The teacher used my paper as an _____ of good handwriting.

8. The mayor will _____ a _____ holiday.

My Spelling Dictation

Write the sentences. Circle the spelling words.

1. _____

_____

2. _____

_____

Word Study

Write the missing letters that make the /l/ sound in these words.

> le   el   al

1. eag_____

2. tow_____

3. speci_____

4. examp_____

5. leg_____

6. who_____

7. sever_____

8. lab_____

9. litt_____

10. terrib_____

Match syllables to make words.
Write the complete words on the lines.

1. spe   quent

2. ques   dress

3. fre   clare

4. in   tion

5. de   cial

6. ad   stead

1. _____

2. _____

3. _____

4. _____

5. _____

6. _____

7. ex   ri   ble

8. sev   e   al

9. ter   e   ple

10. cel   am   brate

11. tel   stru   scope

12. in   er   ment

7. ___example___

8. _____

9. _____

10. _____

11. _____

12. _____

Edit for Spelling

Circle the words that are spelled correctly.

exampel	special	labal
question	declair	address
twole	severul	freqwent
celebrate	telescope	leagle

Circle the misspelled words in the sentences. Write them correctly on the lines.

1. Sevral terible things happened to me yesterday.

   _____ _____

2. I saw an eegle in its nest through my teleskope.

   _____ _____

3. Mom bought a beach towle at a speshul sale.

   _____ _____

4. What is the uddress on the package's lable?

   _____ _____

5. She had a qwestion about which insterment was needed for the operation.

   _____ _____

Building Spelling Skills, Daily Practice • EMC 2709

Spelling List

This Week's Focus:
- Spell words with **ie** and **ei**
- Spell words with the endings **-ing**, **-ed**, **-s**, and **-es**

STEP 1 Read and Spell

STEP 2 Copy and Spell

STEP 3 Cover and Spell

fold

1. tried
2. weigh
3. piece
4. receive
5. their
6. fierce
7. neither
8. field
9. receiving
10. trying
11. hurried
12. siege
13. weighs
14. writing
15. tired
16. having
17. planned
18. worries
19. _____
   bonus word
20. _____
   bonus word

Word Meaning

Homophones are words that sound alike but have
different spellings and different meanings.

1. Write the spelling words that are homophones for these words.

    a. way   _____

    b. there   _____

    c. peace   _____

2. Write the letter in front of the meaning for each word.

    a. neither   _____ intense; savage

    b. siege   _____ a piece of land used for crops or pasture

    c. weigh   _____ one part of a whole thing

    d. field   _____ not either

    e. fierce   _____ to measure how heavy something is

    f. piece   _____ feels concern

    g. worries   _____ surrounding a place in order to capture it

My Spelling Dictation

Write the sentences. Circle the spelling words.

1. _____

    _____

2. _____

    _____

Word Study

Write the words in the correct boxes.

| piece | weigh | tried | field | receive |
| trying | siege | neither | writing | tired |

long **a** sound	long **e** sound	long **i** sound

Add an ending to the base word. Check how you changed the word.

add ing

	no change	drop **e**
1. receive _____		
2. write _____		
3. have _____		
4. try _____		

add ed

	no change	drop **e**	change **y** to **i**	double final consonant
5. receive _____				
6. worry _____				
7. plan _____				
8. hurry _____				

Edit for Spelling

Annie shared her great-grandmother's diary
with her classmates. This entry was written during
the drought on the Eastern Plains of Colorado in 1851.

Circle the 11 misspelled words below.
Write them correctly on the lines.

Worries on the Plains

Dear Diary,

I'm tryin to help during this difficult time. The feerce winds

are laying seige to the carefully planted feilds. We have seen neithur

sun nor rain for seven days. The skies are like a piese of Granny's

pewter. They're gray mood is havving its effect on all of us.

Thomas worrys constantly, and Little Tom is so tarred of the

blowing sand. Will it ever end? I am writting this entry at dusk. As I put

out the lantern tonight, I pray for a gentle rain to wet the soil and sun

to warm the little plants and our spirits.

With a hopeful heart,

Viola

_____   _____   _____

_____   _____   _____

_____   _____   _____

_____   _____

Spelling List

This Week's Focus:
- Spell words with the suffixes -**ness**, -**ist**, and -**ant**
- Spell words with the endings -**ly**, -**er**, -**or**, and -**ar**
- Practice adding suffixes to base words

STEP 1 Read and Spell	STEP 2 Copy and Spell	STEP 3 Cover and Spell

fold

1. kindness

2. darkness

3. happiness

4. loneliness

5. sadness

6. weakness

7. exactly

8. honestly

9. speedily

10. angrily

11. happily

12. friendly

13. especially

14. teacher

15. actor

16. liar

17. biologist

18. assistant

19. _____
    bonus word

20. _____
    bonus word

96

Word Meaning

Complete these tasks using spelling words.

1. What do you call someone who…?

   a. teaches _____

   b. acts _____

   c. tells lies _____

   d. studies living things _____

   e. helps others _____

2. Which of these words describe how something might be done?

   happiness   honestly   exactly

   speedily   assistant   happily

3. Write the letter in front of the meaning for each word.

   a. darkness   _____ specially

   b. loneliness   _____ in an angry manner

   c. especially   _____ absence of light

   d. angrily   _____ having no strength

   e. weakness   _____ feeling alone

My Spelling Dictation

Write the sentences. Circle the spelling words.

1. _____

   _____

2. _____

   _____

Word Study

Add the suffix or ending to each word.
Then circle the words that required a change before adding the suffix or ending.

add **ness**		add **ly**	
1. dark	_____	5. honest	_____
2. lonely	_____	6. angry	_____
3. weak	_____	7. friend	_____
4. happy	_____	8. speedy	_____

Write the base word and the suffix or ending.

	base word	suffix or ending
1. sadness	sad	ness
2. teacher	_____	_____
3. happily	_____	_____
4. kindness	_____	_____
5. exactly	_____	_____
6. liar	_____	_____
7. loneliness	_____	_____
8. actor	_____	_____

Edit for Spelling

Circle the words that are spelled correctly.

lonelyness	biologist	lier	honestly	speedily
kindness	teacher	sadness	happiness	assisstant
exactly	weekness	darkness	espeshully	freindly

Circle the misspelled words in the sentences.
Write them correctly on the lines.

1. That lyer didn't answer the questions honistly.

   _____   _____

2. His new teecher was frindly to all the students.

   _____   _____

3. The biologest's assistent worked speedyly.

   _____   _____   _____

4. Her happyness espeically showed on her face.

   _____   _____

5. An acter must know exacly what to do when the stage is plunged into darknes.

   _____   _____   _____

Spelling List

This Week's Focus:
- Review long vowel sounds
- Review the sounds of /**oo**/ and /**ow**/
- Practice using homophones

STEP 1 Read and Spell	STEP 2 Copy and Spell	STEP 3 Cover and Spell

fold

1. scene
2. they're
3. through
4. heir
5. clothes
6. byte
7. aloud
8. cruise
9. crews
10. isle
11. principal
12. principle
13. hour
14. knew
15. two
16. write
17. chute
18. reign
19. _____ bonus word
20. _____ bonus word

Word Meaning

Complete the crossword puzzle using spelling words.
There are two words <u>not</u> on the spelling list. See if you can figure them out.

Across

1. a group of computer bits
4. the head of a school
10. the period of time a king rules the country
11. a person who inherits property
12. an abbreviation for **submarine**
14. the place where an event or action occurs
16. thoughts expressed vocally are said ____
17. the contraction for **they are**
18. a small island

Down

2. in one end of a tunnel and out the other end
3. garments to wear on the body
5. a steep slide
6. a basic truth or law
7. a period of time
8. a trip by boat from place to place
9. to record thoughts in written form
13. something that makes a ringing sound
15. groups of people working together

My Spelling Dictation

Write the sentences. Circle the spelling words.

1. _____

_____

2. _____

_____

Word Study

Homophones are words that sound alike but have different spellings and different meanings.

Write the spelling words that are homophones for these words.

1. seen _____

2. rain _____

3. threw _____

4. their _____

5. crews _____

6. principle _____

7. right _____

8. air _____

9. allowed _____

10. our _____

11. too _____

12. bite _____

13. I'll _____

14. new _____

15. shoot _____

Write the spelling words in the correct boxes. Listen for the vowel sounds.

chute	scene	aloud	byte	through
clothes	reign	isle	cruise	
write	knew	two	hour	

long **a**	long **e**	long **i**
long **o**	**ow** as in **now**	**oo** as in **too**

102

Edit for Spelling

Circle the 10 misspelled words below.
Write them correctly on the lines.

The Principal and the Principle

Imagine this seen—the princepal in freshly pressed close running threw a fountain of tomato juice. It all happened an our before lunch yesterday.

The kitchen had been closed so that too cruise of electricians could replace some wiring in the cafeteria. Mr. Grant, the principal, was on his way to check their work. Just as he entered the kitchen, the electric can opener buzzed into action. A huge can of tomato juice that had been left on the can opener became the victim of Newton's principel of actions and reactions. The can opener went down; the can was opened, and just as the principal walked in, it flew off the countertop, drenching him in juice.

After much mopping and ten damp towels later, Mr. Grant was ready to walk back to his office. And what about the electricians? Their working on a crews ship heading toward Alaska. I wonder if the ship has a can opener.

_____   _____

_____   _____

_____   _____

_____   _____

_____   _____

Spelling List

This Week's Focus:
- Spell words with the suffixes **-ful**, **-ment**, and **-less**
- Spell multisyllabic words

STEP 1 Read and Spell

STEP 2 Copy and Spell

STEP 3 Cover and Spell

fold

1. thoughtful
2. successful
3. wasteful
4. wonderful
5. skillful
6. plentiful
7. government
8. amusement
9. predicament
10. excitement
11. punishment
12. arrangement
13. fearless
14. careless
15. worthless
16. thoughtless
17. useless
18. reckless
19. _____ bonus word
20. _____ bonus word

104

Word Meaning

Match each spelling word to its meaning.

_____ 1. careless

_____ 2. arrangement

_____ 3. excitement

_____ 4. amusement

_____ 5. fearless

_____ 6. predicament

_____ 7. reckless

_____ 8. punishment

_____ 9. successful

_____ 10. worthless

_____ 11. thoughtful

_____ 12. wonderful

_____ 13. government

_____ 14. wasteful

a. entertainment

b. not paying enough attention

c. to be afraid of nothing

d. marvelous

e. an excited condition

f. an unpleasant or difficult situation

g. a penalty for doing something wrong

h. good-for-nothing

i. to be rash or careless

j. using or spending too much

k. considerate

l. the way in which things are organized

m. the ruling of a country, state, or city

n. having success

My Spelling Dictation

Write the sentences. Circle the spelling words.

1. _____

_____

2. _____

_____

Word Study

Add the correct suffix to the base word.

> **ful** means "full of"   **ment** means "quality or state of"   **less** means "without"

1. The builder's _____ work caused the building to collapse.
   (care)

2. There will be great _____ when the ship lands on Mars.
   (excite)

3. Her _____ behavior made her a popular nurse.
   (thought)

4. That flat ball will be _____ in the basketball game.
   (use)

5. What kind of _____ does Egypt have?
   (govern)

6. Food was _____ at the company picnic.
   (plenty)

Divide these words into syllables. Then circle the suffix.

1. careless   care   (less)

2. wasteful   _____

3. thoughtless   _____

4. plentiful   _____

5. amusement   _____

6. wonderful   _____

7. excitement   _____

8. successful   _____

Edit for Spelling

Circle the words that have the correct suffix.

thoughtment	arrangeful	careless
punishful	thoughtless	worthment
reckless	arrangement	carely
reckful	fearment	excitement
worthless	useful	governless

Circle the misspelled words in the sentences.
Write them correctly on the lines.

1. It is usless to worry about that one carless mistake.

   _____ _____

2. Our arranjment was to meet at the amusment park at 9 o'clock.

   _____ _____

3. Do you think his wreckless behavior deserved such a harsh punichment?

   _____ _____

4. The goverment was finally sucessful in reaching a peaceful solution to

   the pridikament.

   _____ _____ _____

This Week's Focus:
- Spell words with the sound of /sh/ spelled **sh**, **s**, **ci**, **ti**, **ss**, or **si**
- Spell words with the endings **-ian**, **-ion**, and **-tion**

STEP 1 Read and Spell	STEP 2 Copy and Spell	STEP 3 Cover and Spell

fold

1. shoes
2. sure
3. sugar
4. musician
5. patience
6. mission
7. occasion
8. physician
9. tension
10. conclusion
11. constitution
12. caution
13. constellation
14. addition
15. fiction
16. position
17. official
18. glacier
19. _____ bonus word
20. _____ bonus word

Word Meaning

Complete the crossword puzzle using spelling words.
There are two words that are <u>not</u> on the spelling list. See if you can figure them out!

Across

1. urge to be careful
4. a person holding a public office
6. the end
8. a sweet substance
12. a group of stars
13. a mathematical process in which sets are combined
14. a metal container for food
15. coverings for feet
16. a large mass of very slowly moving ice

Down

2. the opposite of **yes**
3. something made up
5. the principles by which a country is governed
7. a person who plays music
9. a doctor
10. the act of waiting without complaining
11. stress or strain
15. without any doubt

My Spelling Dictation

Write the sentences. Circle the spelling words.

1. _____

   _____

2. _____

   _____

Word Study

Circle the letter or letters in each word that make the /sh/ sound.

1. shoes
2. glacier
3. caution
4. sure

5. official
6. addition
7. sugar
8. position

9. mission
10. fiction
11. tension
12. patience

How many different ways was the /sh/ sound spelled? _____

Match syllables to make spelling words.
Write the complete words on the lines.

1. fic   ar   1. _____

2. sug   sion   2. _____

3. pa   tion   3. _____

4. mis   cier   4. _____

5. gla   tience   5. _____

6. phy   clu   cial   6. _____

7. con   fi   tion   7. _____

8. of   di   sion   8. _____

9. ad   si   cian   9. _____

Edit for Spelling

Circle the words that are spelled correctly.

shoes	shure	caution	glacier
fiktion	suger	poisician	musician
mision	official	ocassion	tension

Circle the misspelled words in the sentences. Write them correctly on the lines.

1. Be shure to tie your shoos.

   _____   _____

2. His missun was to study glasher movements.

   _____   _____

3. It takes pacience to become a great musition.

   _____   _____

4. The fysician plays tennis to relieve tenshun.

   _____   _____

5. What was the conclushun of the ficshn story?

   _____   _____

6. His oficial possition is city councilman.

   _____   _____

Spelling List

This Week's Focus:
- Spell words with silent letters
- Review long, short, and schwa vowel sounds

STEP 1 Read and Spell

STEP 2 Copy and Spell

STEP 3 Cover and Spell

fold

1. wrestle
2. wrong
3. answer
4. dough
5. unknown
6. knapsack
7. honor
8. listen
9. climb
10. half
11. island
12. talking
13. design
14. scratch
15. tonight
16. limb
17. knot
18. whistle
19. _____
   bonus word
20. _____
   bonus word

Word Meaning

Answer these questions using spelling words.

1. Which spelling words are the opposites of these words?

   a. right _____   c. whole _____

   b. ask _____   d. speak _____

2. Which spelling words are compound words?

   a. _____   b. _____

3. Which spelling words mean about the same as these words?

   a. incorrect _____   c. scrape _____

   b. respond _____   d. hear _____

4. Add a prefix to make this word mean "not known." _____known

5. Which spelling word means…?

   a. something you make cookies from _____

   b. a piece of land surrounded by water _____

   c. a part of the whole thing _____

   d. to make a sound by blowing through your lips _____

My Spelling Dictation

Write the sentences. Circle the spelling words.

1. _____

   _____

2. _____

   _____

Word Study

Which of the underlined letters are silent?
Circle the silent letters.

1. w̲r̲estle
2. answer
3. honor
4. climb
5. talking
6. knot
7. half
8. whistle
9. tonight
10. island
11. design
12. scratch

Fill in the missing letters to make spelling words.

> mb   kn   wr   st   lf

1. _____ong
2. un_____own
3. li_____en
4. li_____
5. _____apsack
6. _____ot
7. cli_____
8. ha_____

What type of vowel sounds do the underlined letters represent?

	short vowel	long vowel	schwa
1. wrestle	X		
2. scratch			
3. climb			
4. listen			
5. half			
6. answer			
7. dough			
8. knapsack			
9. island			

Edit for Spelling

Circle the 13 misspelled words below.
Write them correctly on the lines.

The Wrong Night to Camp

This summer I went camping on an islend near my home. I carried everything I would need in a napsack. When I reached the ranger station, he was talkin about which campsites were still available for camping tonite. I asked about a campsite near the lake. His anser was to nod his head and point to a trail going up to the left.

I climmed down a slope to the lake. I found a level spot to set up camp. I hung my supplies on a tree limm, using a special not my scout leader had taught me. I pitched my tent, started a fire, and prepared doe for biscuits.

While I waited for the griddle to get hot, I sat on a log and tried to scrach a desine on a chunk of wood. What a peaceful way to spend an afternoon. Then everything started to go wrawng. The sky opened up, and rain slammed down to the ground! I crawled quickly into the tent, but I looked like I had restled a bear in a mud puddle. I hoped the downpour would be over soon. I was hungry for those biscuits!

_____   _____   _____

_____   _____   _____

_____   _____   _____

_____   _____

Spelling List

This Week's Focus:
- Spell words with the prefixes **re-**, **dis-**, **mis-**, and **il-**
- Practice adding prefixes to base words

STEP 1 Read and Spell

STEP 2 Copy and Spell

STEP 3 Cover and Spell

fold

1. rewrite
2. reappear
3. recall
4. recover
5. rebuild
6. dishonest
7. disagree
8. disappear
9. disappoint
10. disconnect
11. disapprove
12. misbehave
13. misfortune
14. misunderstand
15. misspell
16. misuse
17. illegal
18. illegible
19. _____ bonus word
20. _____ bonus word

Word Meaning

Write the spelling word that means...

1. not neat enough to read _____

2. to spell incorrectly _____

3. to fail to satisfy a wish or need _____

4. to build something again _____

5. bad luck _____

6. to use something incorrectly _____

7. to write again _____

8. to not agree _____

9. to behave badly _____

10. not legal _____

11. to come into view again _____

12. to be no longer seen _____

13. to get back _____

My Spelling Dictation

Write the sentences. Circle the spelling words.

1. _____

_____

2. _____

_____

Word Study

Add the correct prefix to the base word.

re	dis	mis	il

1. Dad did not wish to _____ the children, so he rushed to get to
   (appoint)

   the game on time.

2. We promised Mother we wouldn't _____ at the pool.
   (behave)

3. Many people had to _____ their homes after the hurricane.
   (build)

4. It is _____ to drive a car without a license.
   (legal)

5. Did you _____ the directions for last night's homework?
   (understand)

6. My allowance seems to _____ as soon as I get it!
   (appear)

7. You need to _____ your report so I can read it.
   (write)

Add a prefix to make each base word into its opposite.

1. honest _____dishonest_____

2. agree _____

3. legal _____

4. approve _____

5. legible _____

6. connect _____

118

Edit for Spelling

Circle the words that have the correct prefix.

recover	dislegible	misappear	disappoint
disfortune	rebehave	illegal	illegible
ilbuild	disfortune	dishonest	ilspell
reunderstand	recall	misconnect	disapprove

Circle the misspelled words in the sentences.
Write them correctly on the lines.

1. The town had to rebiuld both homes and businesses after the terrible

   misfortunate brought on by the tornado.

   _____   _____

2. Do you rekall how to disconect the TV?

   _____   _____

3. The principal will desapprove if we missbehave in school.

   _____   _____

4. If you mispell words and use ilegible handwriting, you will have to reright

   your story.

   _____   _____   _____   _____

Building Spelling Skills

Spelling List

This Week's Focus:
- Spell words with the /**f**/ sound

STEP 1 Read and Spell	STEP 2 Copy and Spell	STEP 3 Cover and Spell

fold

1. paragraph
2. trophy
3. nephew
4. enough
5. cough
6. fourth
7. Friday
8. physical
9. roughest
10. pharmacy
11. fragile
12. fluid
13. briefly
14. festival
15. stuffed
16. triumph
17. telephone
18. few
19. _____ bonus word
20. _____ bonus word

Word Meaning

Complete the crossword puzzle using spelling words.

Down

1. the son of your brother or sister
3. pertaining to the body
4. a celebration
6. as much as is needed
7. an award, often in the form of a statue or cup
8. easily broken
9. an ordinal number

Across

2. a group of sentences about the same idea
5. an instrument for talking between two distant points
8. not many
10. a drugstore
11. to force air from your lungs with a sudden effort and noise
12. success or victory
13. in a short manner

My Spelling Dictation

Write the sentences. Circle the spelling words.

1. _____

   _____

2. _____

   _____

Fill in the blanks with letters that make the /**f**/ sound.

> f   ph   gh

1. paragra_____

2. _____ew

3. tro_____y

4. tele_____one

5. enou_____

6. ne_____ew

7. brie_____ly

8. rou_____est

9. _____armacy

10. _____estival

11. cou_____

12. stuf_____ed

13. _____luid

14. _____ysical

15. _____ragile

16. trium_____

Write the spelling word that is a synonym for each word.

1. award   _____

2. plenty   _____

3. drugstore   _____

4. liquid   _____

5. delicate   _____

6. handful   _____

7. victory   _____

8. shortly   _____

Write the spelling word that is a synonym for the words in parentheses.

1. She received a _____ after her great _____.
        (award)   (victory)

2. Mrs. Wu bought a _____ teacup from the _____.
        (delicate)   (drugstore)

3. The host spoke _____ after the guests had eaten _____.
        (shortly)   (plenty)

Edit for Spelling

Circle the 12 misspelled words below.
Write them correctly on the lines.

The Brief Triumph

From my bed I saw the trophee sitting on my desk. I smiled.

It had been a triumf followed by a disaster. It all happened last Fridey.

I went with my neffew to the Obon Festtival. We were to compete in

a kendo competition. The crowd that had gathered loved those

phisical duels.

Wearing traditional dress, the competitors moved like frajle dancers

around the ring. Breefly lunging toward each other and then stepping

back, the competitors performed. It was one of the ruffest contests

we had entered, and we were lucky enuf to win.

As the trophy was presented, we bowed and stepped from the

stage. I tripped on the forth step and fell—triumph followed by disaster.

The graceful warrior is now grounded for a phew weeks with a broken ankle!

_____   _____   _____

_____   _____   _____

_____   _____   _____

_____   _____   _____

Spelling List

This Week's Focus:
- Spell words with the prefixes **im-**, **in-**, **pre-**, and **un-**

STEP 1 Read and Spell	STEP 2 Copy and Spell	STEP 3 Cover and Spell

fold

1. imperfect

2. impolite

3. impatient

4. improper

5. inactive

6. inconvenient

7. incorrect

8. inconsiderate

9. preview

10. prejudice

11. prevent

12. prefix

13. prehistoric

14. unable

15. uncertain

16. uncomfortable

17. unaware

18. ungrateful

19. _____
   bonus word

20. _____
   bonus word

Fill in the blanks with spelling words.

1. A small crack made the cup _____.

2. It is _____ to always take the largest piece.

3. Bears are _____ during the cold winter months.

4. Our teacher was _____ when she was _____
   to keep the class on task.

5. He was _____ that his _____ behavior

   made other people feel _____.

6. Professor Singh will _____ that new book about

   _____ animals before using it in his class.

7. The _____ I wrote before a base word was _____

   and changed the meaning of my sentence.

8. How can we _____ _____ against others

   from happening?

My Spelling Dictation

Write the sentences. Circle the spelling words.

1. _____

   _____

2. _____

   _____

Word Study

Add the correct prefix to each base word. Write **im**, **in**, **pre**, or **un**.

1. not perfect   _____perfect

2. judgment without knowledge   _____judice

3. contains mistakes   _____correct

4. not sure   _____certain

5. to inspect beforehand   _____view

6. to keep from happening   _____vent

7. causing difficulty   _____convenient

8. comes before a word to change its meaning   _____fix

9. not conscious   _____aware

10. lacking good manners   _____polite

Write the spelling word that is an antonym for each word.

1. perfect _____

2. polite _____

3. aware _____

4. active _____

5. grateful _____

6. patient _____

7. considerate _____

8. historic _____

9. comfortable _____

10. convenient _____

11. able _____

12. proper _____

Edit for Spelling

Circle the words that have the correct prefix.

inpolite	uncorrect	prevent
unaware	inconsiderate	unview
prehistoric	unproper	uncertain
preactive	inconvenient	inable
unpatient	imperfect	ingrateful
prejudice	incomfortable	prefix

Circle the misspelled words in the sentences.
Write them correctly on the lines.

1. The words impolight and inkonsiderate have about the same meaning.

   _____   _____

2. We went to a prevue showing of a new movie about life in perhistoric times.

   _____   _____

3. The test made him uncomterble because he was unsertain about how to do

   the math problems.

   _____   _____

4. I was unawear that my telephone perfix had been changed from 408 to 412.

   _____   _____

This Week's Focus:
- Spell words with Greek and Latin roots and affixes

STEP 1 Read and Spell

STEP 2 Copy and Spell

STEP 3 Cover and Spell

fold

1. geology
2. geometry
3. geography
4. geologist
5. action
6. enact
7. transport
8. import
9. portable
10. bicycle
11. cyclone
12. encyclopedia
13. autograph
14. automobile
15. automatic
16. autobiography
17. telegraph
18. photograph
19. _____
   bonus word
20. _____
   bonus word

Word Meaning

Complete the crossword puzzle using spelling words.

Across

1. a person who studies geology
4. a two-wheeled vehicle
6. a violent windstorm
9. a self-written story of your life
12. a passenger vehicle powered by an engine
13. a device for sending coded messages over wires
14. to make into law

Down

2. the study of the Earth's surface, climate, and people
3. to carry from one place to another
5. a set of books giving information
7. easily carried
8. something being done
10. a picture made with a camera
11. to bring something in from another country

My Spelling Dictation

Write the sentences. Circle the spelling words.

1. _____

_____

2. _____

_____

Use these word parts to help you make spelling words.

geo = earth	**cycle** = circle	**auto** = self	**ology** = study of
act = do	**photo** = light	**trans** = across	**tion** = state of being
bio = life	**port** = carry	**bi** = two	**graph** = write

Which word parts make words meaning...?

1. "the study of the earth"

   ___geo___ + ___ology___ = ___geology___

2. "writing of the story of yourself"

   _____ + _____ + _____ + y = _____

3. "carry something across a distance"

   _____ + _____ = _____

4. "record using light"

   _____ + _____ = _____

5. "doing something"

   _____ + _____ = _____

6. "having two wheels"

   _____ + _____ = _____

Edit for Spelling

Circle the word in each row that is spelled correctly.

1. inact   enact   in act

2. cyclone   cyclon   syclone

3. bicyle   bicylcle   bicycle

4. fotograph   photograf   photograph

Circle the 10 misspelled words below. Write them correctly on the lines.

My Friend, Frank

Frank is better than an automatick encylopydia. If you ask him about anything, he always has the answer. I needed help finding Malaysia. No problem—Frank is good at geogruphy. My dad's car sounded strange. No problem—Frank understands automobeles. He helped my sister with her geomtrie, my mother with geollogy, and my grandfather with his autobiografy. No problem! Frank is my own special portabel library. He helps me emport and transprot information. "Frank" is what I named my new computer!

_____   _____   _____

_____   _____   _____

_____   _____

Spelling List

This Week's Focus:
- Spell multisyllabic verbs
- Spell words with the suffix -**tion**

STEP 1 Read and Spell

STEP 2 Copy and Spell

STEP 3 Cover and Spell

fold

1. destruct
2. destruction
3. describe
4. description
5. decorate
6. decoration
7. divide
8. division
9. administer
10. administration
11. populate
12. population
13. infect
14. infection
15. punctuate
16. punctuation
17. attend
18. attention
19. _____
   bonus word
20. _____
   bonus word

Word Meaning

Fill in the blanks with spelling words.

1. Aunt Jill is going to _____ my birthday cake.

   She always makes a beautiful _____.

2. Be sure to _____ your story correctly.

   I am going to check your _____ skills.

3. Please _____ your favorite place to read.

   Write a brief _____ of that place.

4. Who was hired to _____ that special project?

   The college _____ hired three people to do the job.

5. In the 1800s, people were encouraged to _____ the western

   territories. Today, many western cities have a large _____.

My Spelling Dictation

Write the sentences. Circle the spelling words.

1. _____

   _____

2. _____

   _____

Word Study

Add the suffix **tion** or **sion** to change these verbs to nouns.
Some spelling changes will be needed.

1. destruct _____

2. infect _____

3. attend _____

4. describe _____

5. decorate _____

6. administer _____

7. populate _____

8. divide _____

9. punctuate _____

Divide these words into syllables.

1. destruct _____ de _____ struct _____

2. divide _____

3. description _____

4. decorate _____

5. infection _____

6. populate _____

7. punctuate _____

8. attention _____

9. administer _____

10. decoration _____

11. punctuation _____

Edit for Spelling

Circle the words that are spelled correctly.

disstruction	description	decorate
attention	puntuashun	populat
admenister	infection	administration
dekoration	divizion	enfect
uttend	describe	population
punctuate	devide	destruct

Circle the misspelled words in the sentences.
Write them correctly on the lines.

1. Can you discribe the decorashun on the banner?

   _____   _____

2. The owner plans to devide the admenestration of his company into three departments.

   _____   _____

3. Pay atention as you write your story so that the spelling and puntuation are correct.

   _____   _____

4. Ten percent of the populacian was infectted with measles.

   _____   _____

This Week's Focus:
- Spell multisyllabic words

STEP 1 Read and Spell

STEP 2 Copy and Spell

STEP 3 Cover and Spell

fold

1. multiply
2. temperature
3. vertical
4. equation
5. currency
6. amphibian
7. intersection
8. environment
9. agriculture
10. frequency
11. civilization
12. manufacture
13. characteristic
14. atmosphere
15. representative
16. semicircle
17. substitute
18. technology
19. _____ bonus word
20. _____ bonus word

Word Meaning

Write the spelling word that means…

1. straight up and down   _____

2. a member of a group of coldblooded
   animals with moist skin and a backbone   _____

3. the place where one thing crosses another   _____

4. the raising of crops and farm animals   _____

5. the rate at which something happens   _____

6. half a circle   _____

7. the money used in a country   _____

8. the gases surrounding the Earth   _____

9. the culture of a people or period of time   _____

10. something used in place of another thing   _____

11. a mathematical statement that shows two
    quantities are equal   _____

12. a measurement of the degree of heat or cold   _____

My Spelling Dictation

Write the sentences. Circle the spelling words.

1. _____

   _____

2. _____

   _____

Word Study

Fill in the missing syllables to make spelling words.

1. mul_____ply

2. verti_____

3. e_____tion

4. _____rency

5. fre_____cy

6. atmos_____

7. _____stitute

8. am_____ian

9. agri_____ture

10. _____icir_____

11. _____nology

12. tempera_____

13. _____acter_____tic

14. in_____sec_____

15. en_____ron_____

16. repre_____a_____

17. _____iliza_____

18. man_____ _____ture

Count the number of syllables in these words.
Write the words in the correct boxes.

temperature	vertical	amphibian	intersection	manufacture
environment	agriculture	civilization	multiply	representative
characteristic	atmosphere	semicircle	technology	
substitute	currency	frequency	equation	

3 syllables	4 syllables	5 syllables

138

Edit for Spelling

Circle the misspelled words in the sentences.
Write them correctly on the lines.

1. Can an amfibian live in an envirunment where the temperachur is very low?

   _____   _____   _____

2. The math equasion required me to mulltiply fractions.

   _____   _____

3. That prehistoric civilisation had advanced to a stage where agrikulture was important.

   _____   _____

4. What kind of atmusphere is characturistic of Venus?

   _____   _____

5. The government representuteves stood in a semycircle around the new monument.

   _____   _____

6. You will need to substutute English pounds for your American kurrency when
   you visit Great Britain.

   _____   _____

7. His company will manufacter stop signs to place at the intersecton of Main Street
   and Fifth Avenue.

   _____   _____

Spelling Record Sheet

Building Spelling Skills

Students' Names																
1																
2																
3																
4																
5																
6																
7																
8																
9																
10																
11																
12																
13																
14																
15																
16																
17																
18																
19																
20																
21																
22																
23																
24																
25																
26																
27																
28																
29																
30																

Note: Reproduce this form twice for each student to track his or her progress.

My Spelling Record

Spelling List	Date	Number Correct	Words Missed

Spelling Test

Building Spelling Skills

Listen to the words.
Write each word on a line.

1. _____   11. _____

2. _____   12. _____

3. _____   13. _____

4. _____   14. _____

5. _____   15. _____

6. _____   16. _____

7. _____   17. _____

8. _____   18. _____

9. _____   19. _____

10. _____   20. _____

Listen to the sentences.
Write them on the lines.

1. _____

_____

_____

2. _____

_____

_____

Building Spelling Skills

Spelling List

STEP 1 Read and Spell	STEP 2 Copy and Spell	STEP 3 Cover and Spell
1.		
2.		
3.		
4.		
5.		
6.		
7.		
8.		
9.		
10.		
11.		
12.		
13.		
14.		
15.		
16.		
17.		
18.		
19.		
20.		

fold

143   Building Spelling Skills, Daily Practice • EMC 2709

Note: Reproduce this form to make your own crossword puzzles.

Crossword Puzzle

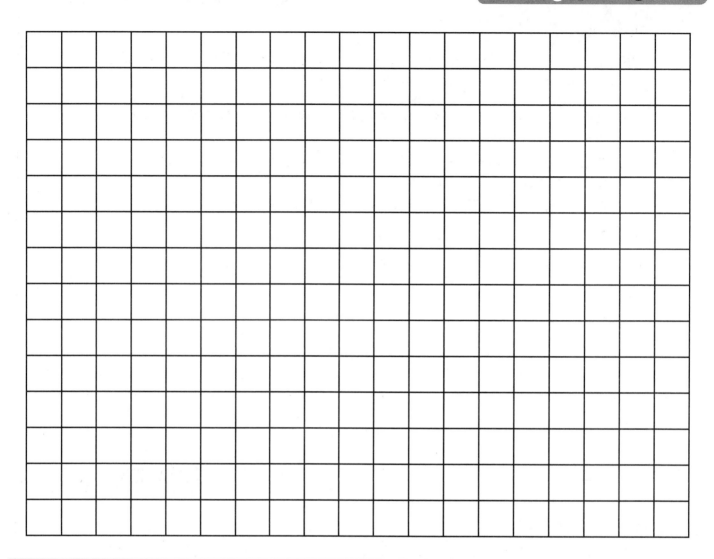

Across	Down

Building Spelling Skills

Dear Parents,

Attached is your child's spelling list for this week. Encourage him or her to practice the words in one or more of these ways:

1. Read and spell each word. Cover it up and write it. Uncover the word and check to see if it is correct.
2. Find the words on the spelling list in printed materials such as books and magazines.
3. Read a word aloud and ask your child to spell it (either aloud or written on paper).

Thank you for your support of our spelling program.

Sincerely,

Building Spelling Skills

Dear Parents,

Attached is your child's spelling list for this week. Encourage him or her to practice the words in one or more of these ways:

1. Read and spell each word. Cover it up and write it. Uncover the word and check to see if it is correct.
2. Find the words on the spelling list in printed materials such as books and magazines.
3. Read a word aloud and ask your child to spell it (either aloud or written on paper).

Thank you for your support of our spelling program.

Sincerely,

Student Spelling Dictionaries

Self-made spelling dictionaries provide students with a reference for the spelling of words they frequently use in their writing.

Materials

- copy of "My Own Spelling Dictionary" form (page 147)
- 26 sheets of lined paper—6" x 9" (15 x 23 cm)
- 2 sheets of construction paper or tagboard for cover—6" x 9" (15 x 23 cm)
- crayons or markers
- glue
- stapler
- masking tape

Steps to Follow

1 Color and cut out the cover sheet form. Glue it to the front cover of the dictionary.

2 Staple the lined paper inside the cover. Place masking tape over the staples.

3 Guide students (or ask parent volunteers) to write a letter of the alphabet on each page.

What to Include

1. When students ask for the correct spelling of a special word, have them write it in their dictionary.

2. Include special words being learned as part of science or social studies units.

3. Include words for special holidays.

4. Include the common words students continue to misspell on tests and in daily written work.

My Own

Spelling Dictionary

Name _____

Building Spelling Skills

My Own

Spelling Dictionary

Name _____

Master Word List

able	autobiography	choose	diagram	explain	guarding
about	autograph	chute	dictionary	families	guesses
action	automatic	circle	didn't	fault	half
actor	automobile	city	different	favorite	happen
addition	avoid	civilization	disagree	fearless	happily
address	awful	climb	disappear	fences	happiness
addresses	awhile	clothes	disappoint	festival	haul
administer	awkward	clue	disapprove	few	haven't
administration	awoke	collar	disconnect	fiction	having
afraid	baby-sit	color	dishonest	field	height
again	beautiful	communicate	divide	fierce	heir
agriculture	because	compare	division	fifteen	hello
airmail	been	concert	doctor	figure	high school
algebra	before	conclusion	does	finished	higher
all right	began	constellation	doesn't	first aid	himself
allow	beginning	constitution	dollar	flashlight	honestly
along	belong	copy	don't	flies	honor
aloud	beware	cough	dough	fluid	hour
already	bicycle	could	dozen	followed	house
although	biologist	couldn't	drawn	force	hurried
always	birthday	countries	duty	fourth	I'll
amount	bodyguard	country	eager	fragile	I'm
amphibian	boundary	cousin	eagle	freight	I've
amusement	bragged	crews	early	frequency	idea
angrily	bridge	cruise	earth	frequent	illegal
animal	briefly	cube	easily	Friday	illegible
annoy	broken	currency	echo	friendly	impatient
another	brought	cute	ecology	friends	imperfect
answer	bulletin	cyclone	electric	friendship	impolite
anything	businesses	dairy	employ	fuel	import
apply	buy	dancing	enact	future	important
approach	byte	dangerous	encyclopedia	generous	improper
April	called	daring	energy	genius	inactive
area	calves	darkness	enough	geography	inconsiderate
aren't	camera	daughter	environment	geologist	inconvenient
argument	careless	daybreak	equation	geology	incorrect
arithmetic	carried	decided	equator	geometry	infect
arrangement	caution	declare	especially	glacier	infection
article	celebrate	decorate	everybody	gloomy	inquire
assistant	certain	decoration	everyone	goal	instead
athletes	characteristic	describe	exactly	goalkeeper	instrument
atmosphere	cherries	description	example	good-bye	intersection
attend	children	design	exchange	government	island
attention	chocolates	destruct	excitement	ground	isle
author	choice	destruction	exciting	grudge	isn't

it's	nephew	prefix	royal	talking	umpire
January	nice	prehistoric	ruin	teacher	unable
kindness	o'clock	prejudice	sadness	technology	unaware
knapsack	obey	prevent	scene	telegraph	uncertain
knew	occasion	preview	school	telephone	uncomfortable
knight	ocean	principal	scratch	telescope	understood
knot	off	principle	second	temperature	ungrateful
label	office	program	segment	tension	universe
laid	official	punctuate	semicircle	terrible	unknown
large	oldest	punctuation	several	their	until
laughed	once	puncture	shoes	themselves	unusual
lawyer	one-way	punishment	should	there's	urgent
leaves	only	purchases	siege	they	useless
lecture	orchestra	purpose	signal	they're	usually
legal	ordinary	python	silent	they've	variety
length	other	quarter	since	thirsty	vertical
lessons	ounce	question	skiing	though	very
liar	ourselves	quickest	skillful	thought	wasteful
license	outside	quiet	skis	thoughtful	watches
limb	owner	quite	sleigh	thoughtless	we're
listen	oxygen	radio	smiling	thousand	weaker
little	oyster	raise	smuggler	threw	weakness
lives	paragraph	ready	somehow	throat	weigh
lonelier	partner	reappear	something	through	weighs
loneliness	patience	rebuild	special	thumb	where
loose	payment	recall	speedily	Thursday	which
loving	peaceful	receive	spoil	tiniest	whistle
lying	people	receiving	spoken	tired	white
manufacture	person	reckless	sprout	together	who's
maybe	pharmacy	recover	square	tomorrow	whole
mayor	photograph	referee	stalk	tonight	whose
misbehave	physical	region	stare	towel	widest
misfortune	physician	regular	station	trace	women
mission	pictures	reign	straight	trading	won't
misspell	piece	relation	studied	transport	wonder
misunderstand	planned	remember	stuffed	traveling	wonderful
misuse	please	representative	stunt	tried	worried
moisture	plentiful	rewrite	substitute	triumph	worries
months	poem	rhyme	successful	trophy	worthless
mountain	populate	rhythm	sudden	trouble	wrestle
multiply	population	roofs	sugar	truth	write
musician	portable	rookie	sure	truthful	writing
myself	position	rough	surprise	trying	wrong
neighborhood	potato	roughest	surrounded	Tuesday	wrote
neither	predicament	route	swimming	two	you're

You are a SUPER SPELLER!

Super Speller

Name

Congratulations!!

Answer Key

Page 21
1. oxygen, until
2. cousin, grudge, umpire
3. thumb, stunt
4. another, city
5. sudden, began, very
6. copy, trouble
7. which

Page 22
rough   thumb   trouble
grudge   Once   cousin
stunt   another   until
sudden   does   umpire

1. begăn
2. ŏppŏsĭte
3. ănŏther
4. cŏpy
5. ŭmpire
6. which
7. cĭty
8. ŭntĭl

1. trou — ble — 1. trouble
2. cou — sin — 2. cousin
3. be — gan — 3. began
4. cop — y — 4. copy
5. un — til — 5. until
6. um — pire — 6. umpire
7. sud — den — 7. sudden
8. cit — y — 8. city

Page 23
These words should be circled:
1. grudge
2. another
3. does
4. trouble
5. cousin
6. oxygen
7. umpire
8. city
9. until
10. which
11. thumb
12. very

These words should be circled and written correctly:
1. Cuzin / Unother / Sity
   cousin another city
2. Oxigin / Entil / Begun
   oxygen until began
3. Wunce / Truble / Stunts
   Once trouble stunt
4. Duz / Verie / Ruff
   Does very rough

Page 25
Across
1. radio
5. payment
7. relation
8. sleigh
10. afraid
11. freight
13. station
14. daybreak
16. laid

Down
2. April
3. favorite
4. straight
6. explain
7. raise
9. height
12. trace
15. able

Page 26
1. payment
2. raise
3. they
4. able
5. relation
6. afraid
7. sleigh
8. straight
9. favorite
10. radio
11. daybreak
12. explain
13. laid
14. April
15. trace
16. freight
17. station
18. height

1. 2
2. 2
3. 2
4. 2
5. 1
6. 1
7. 1
8. 3
9. 1
10. 2
11. 2
12. 1
13. 2
14. 1
15. 3
16. 1
17. 3
18. 1

Page 27
These words should be circled:
1. payment
2. height
3. afraid
4. relation
5. daybreak
6. laid
7. favorite
8. April
9. radio
10. explain
11. straight
12. raise

These words should be circled and written correctly:
1. Aprul / faverute
   April favorite
2. paiment / Slay
   payment sleigh
3. explane / radeo
   explain radio
4. layed / straite / frayt
   laid straight freight

Page 29
1. fifteen, eager or ready, referee
2. Please, cube, unusual or beautiful or cute
3. fuel, ready, universe
4. easily, beautiful or unusual
5. communicate, ecology, future
6. Only, been

Page 30

long **e**	long **u**
fifteen	cube
eager	universe
referee	future
easily	communicate
ready	fuel
please	cute
maybe	unusual
only	beautiful
ecology	

1. 3
2. 3
3. 2
4. 4
5. 1
6. 4
7. 2
8. 3
9. 4
10. 1
11. 3
12. 2
13. 2
14. 2

Page 31
These words should be circled:
1. eager
2. ready
3. cute
4. been
5. please
6. beautiful
7. fuel
8. easily
9. future
10. maybe
11. fifteen
12. cube

These words should be circled and written correctly:
1. Plez / fiftene / reddy
   Please fifteen ready
2. refree / Comunikate / ownlee
   referee communicate only
3. eegir / unuzual / kube
   eager unusual cube
4. bin / fewl
   been fuel

Page 33
1. a. throat   c. goal
   b. oldest   d. owner
2. b f a e c g d

3. a. obey   d. awoke
    b. hello   e. followed
    c. approach   f. broken

Page 34
1. obey   9. hello
2. goal   10. approach
3. program   11. broken
4. throat   12. spoken
5. poem   13. wrote
6. ocean   14. owner
7. tomorrow   15. potato
8. oldest   16. awoke

1. past   7. present
2. past   8. past
3. present   9. present
4. past   10. past
5. past   11. present
6. past   12. present

1. followed   3. broke
2. wrote   4. awoke

Page 35
These words should be circled:
1. obey   7. goal
2. ocean   8. potato
3. poem   9. tomorrow
4. owner   10. program
5. approach   11. throat
6. wrote   12. awoke

These words should be circled
and written correctly:
1. gole   oshun   tomorro
   goal   ocean   tomorrow
2. oldist   obay
   oldest   obey
3. borken   putato   throte
   broken   potato   throat
4. onner   rote   pome
   owner   wrote   poem

Page 37
1. it's
2. couldn't, didn't or doesn't
3. don't, aren't
4. Who's, o'clock

1. they have   5. is not
2. we are   6. have not
3. you are   7. does not
4. I have   8. there is

Page 38
1. I'll   w i
2. haven't   o
3. we're   a
4. they've   h a
5. couldn't   o
6. you're   a
7. there's   i
8. doesn't   o
9. it's   i
10. I've   h a
11. who's   i
12. don't   o

1. they're   5. wasn't
2. we'll   6. they'll
3. wouldn't   7. hasn't
4. she's   8. he's

who's, whose

Page 39
1. I'll   6. it's   11. they've
2. won't   7. didn't   12. don't
3. o'clock   8. aren't   13. we're
4. doesn't   9. you're   14. isn't
5. there's   10. haven't   15. couldn't

These words should be circled
and written correctly:
1. Culdn't
   Couldn't
2. Who's
   Whose
3. Ive   oclock
   I've   o'clock
4. Theyv'e   did'nt
   They've   didn't
5. Were   Wo'nt
   We're   Won't
6. Ill   whose
   I'll   who's

Page 41
Down   **Across**
1. silent   2. smiling
4. inquire   3. license
5. quite   6. knight
7. higher   9. idea
8. variety   11. rhyme
10. lying   12. widest
             13. diagram
             14. python

Page 42
1. lying   10. smiling
2. idea   11. knight
3. silent   12. quite
4. python   13. variety
5. widest   14. I'm
6. rhyme   15. buy
7. myself   16. higher
8. apply   17. license
9. diagram   18. inquire

1. lying
2. smiling
3. inquire
4. buy
5. apply
6. higher
7. widest

Page 43
These words should be circled:
rhyme   myself
python   idea
lying   diagram

These words should be circled
and written correctly:
1. knite   diagarm
   knight   diagram
2. miself   smileng   silunt
   myself   smiling   silent
3. pyton   hier
   python   higher
4. quit   ime
   quite   rhyme
5. Im   bye   varitee
   I'm   buy   variety

Page 45
1. a. could or should   d. duty
   b. school   e. rookie
   c. threw or clue   f. truth

2. a. gloomy   g. choose
   b. threw   h. clue
   c. rookie   i. truth
   d. ruin   j. bulletin
   e. route   k. understood
   f. loose   l. usually

Page 46

look	too
rookie	gloomy
understood	school
neighborhood	loose
could	choose
should	route
bulletin	clue
	truth
	duty
	threw
	ruin
	Tuesday
	usually

1. gloom — ie   1. gloomy
2. rook — in   2. rookie
3. du — y   3. duty
4. ru — day   4. ruin
5. Tues — ty   5. Tuesday

Page 47

These words should be circled:

school   bulletin
rookie   usually
truth   ruin

These words should be circled and written correctly:

1. gloome   rooin
   gloomy   ruin
2. klew   trooth
   clue   truth
3. nayberhood   usully   skool
   neighborhood usually school
4. thru   ruky
   threw   rookie
5. undrestood   bulliten   Tusday
   understood   bulletin Tuesday

Page 49

1. Moisture, mountain
2. oyster, spoil
3. ounce, amount
4. allow, annoy
5. royal, employ
6. sprout, boundary, house
7. avoid, ground
8. choice, ourselves

Page 50

1. choice   9. ground
2. royal   10. house
3. spoil   11. boundary
4. avoid   12. allow
5. employ   13. mountain
6. moisture   14. ourselves
7. oyster   15. somehow
8. annoy   16. ounce

1. a void   6. moun tain
2. oys ter   7. our selves
3. roy al   8. al low
4. em ploy   9. some how
5. an noy   10. a mount

Page 51

These words should be circled:

1. spoil   6. amount
2. royal   7. somehow
3. avoid   8. ourselves
4. oyster   9. annoy
5. ounce   10. boundary

These words should be circled and written correctly:

1. enploy   howse
   employ   house
2. choyse   mountin
   choice   mountain
3. moysture   grownd
   moisture   ground
4. sumhow   ownce   umount
   Somehow   ounce   amount

Page 53

1. a. baby-sit, one-way, or good-bye
   b. first aid, high school, or all right
   c. flashlight, goalkeeper, airmail, bodyguard, something, birthday, outside, everybody, everyone, anything, themselves, or himself
2. goalkeeper, bodyguard, everybody, everyone, themselves, himself
3. first aid
4. everybody, everyone
5. a. good-bye
   b. something or anything
   c. outside
   d. everybody or everyone

Page 54

outside, birthday, high school, good-bye, himself, something, all right, airmail

1. first aid   a
2. flashlight   i
3. one-way   a
4. everyone   e
5. maybe   a   e
6. anything   e
7. baby-sit   a   e

Page 55

These words should be circled:

1. baby-sit   6. one-way
2. first aid   7. birthday
3. flashlight   8. good-bye
4. all right   9. anything
5. airmail   10. high school

These words should be circled and written correctly:

1. first-ade   goal keeper
   first aid   goalkeeper
2. allright   birth day   air-mail
   all right   birthday   airmail
3. bodygard   flashlite
   bodyguard   flashlight
4. Evrybody   out side
   Everybody   outside

Page 57

1. daughter, awful
2. author, drawn
3. lawyer, already, office
4. always, brought
5. called, because
6. fault, off
7. awkward, stalk

Page 58

1. stalk   9. office
2. off   10. although
3. because   11. awkward
4. brought   12. already
5. called   13. daughter
6. drawn   14. lawyer
7. haul   15. author
8. belong

1. awful   5. always
2. awkward   6. belong
3. fault   7. haul
4. author   8. off

1. awkward, awful
2. author, always
3. haul, off

Page 59
These words should be circled and written correctly:

lawyer   called   because
daughter   office   brought
awkward   awful   drawn
fault   always

Page 61
1. surrounded   carried
   studied   worried
   bragged   finished
   laughed
2. skiing, swimming, or traveling
3. a. finished   e. quickest
    b. traveling   f. laughed
    c. weaker   g. bragged
    d. worried   h. tiniest

Page 62
1. laughing—no change
2. loving—drop **e**
3. beginning—double final
                consonant
4. skiing—no change
5. swimming—double final
                consonant

1. surrounded—no change
2. studied—change **y** to **i**
3. traded—drop **e**
4. carried—change **y** to **i**
5. excited—drop **e**

1. quickest   3. weaker
2. lonelier   4. tiniest

Page 63
These words should be circled:
1. loving
2. lonelier
3. surrounded
4. trading

These words should be circled and written correctly:

bragged   skiing   laughed
beginning   exciting   worried
traveling   quickest   finished

Page 65
Down
1. countries
2. calves
3. guesses
5. lessons
7. fences
9. friends
10. families
11. lives
13. roofs

Across
4. women
5. leaves
6. addresses
8. people
12. skis
14. cherries
15. flies
16. businesses

Page 66
1. skis—add **s**
2. countries—change **y** to **i** and add **es**
3. fences—add **s**
4. leaves—change **f** to **v** and add **es**
5. roofs—add **s**
6. flies—change **y** to **i** and add **es**
7. lives—change **f** to **v** and add **es**
8. families—change **y** to **i** and add **es**
9. guesses—add **es**
10. pictures—add **s**
11. calves—change **f** to **v** and add **es**
12. lessons—add **s**
13. businesses—add **es**
14. friends—add **s**
15. cherries—change **y** to **i** and add **es**
16. addresses—add **es**

women   people

Page 67
These words should be circled:
addresses, lessons, friends, leaves, fences, families, businesses, addresses, roofs

These words should be circled and written correctly:
1. (womun) (lessuns) (peopel)
   women   lessons   people
2. (adresses) (frends) (countrys)
   addresses   friends   countries

3. (busnesses) (pitchers) (familees)
   businesses   pictures   families
4. (calfs)   (cherrys)
   calves   cherries

Page 69
Across
1. thirsty
3. purpose
6. smuggler
7. mayor
8. person
10. earth
11. dollar
12. camera
13. collar
14. color
15. wonder

Down
2. surprise
4. remember
5. Thursday
9. certain
11. doctor
13. cold

Non-spelling word is **cold**

Page 70
1. urgent
2. thirsty
3. collar
4. camera
5. wonder
6. doctor
7. Thursday
8. earth
9. certain
10. color
11. purpose
12. mayor
13. smuggler
14. surprise
15. person
16. dollar
17. early

1. ur
2. thirst
3. won
4. smug
5. pur
6. col
7. cer
8. may
9. ear
10. sur

1. urgent
2. thirsty
3. wonder
4. smuggler
5. purpose
6. collar
7. certain
8. mayor
9. early
10. surprise

Page 71
1. urgent   6. mayor
2. camera   7. person
3. earth   8. doctor
4. dollar   9. early
5. wonder   10. color

These words should be circled and written correctly:
1. (mayir) (erly) (Thirsday)
   mayor early Thursday
2. (irgent) (thirstee)
   urgent thirsty
3. (cirtain) (docter)
   certain doctor
4. (persun) (remembre) (perpose)
   person remember purpose
5. (smuggla) (kamera) (doller)
   smuggler camera dollar

Page 73
1. dictionary
2. dairy
3. a. orchestra
   b. partner
4. a. beware   d. guarding
   b. daring   e. force
   c. argument
5. a. large   c. ordinary
   b. before
6. a. square   d. large
   b. daring   e. force
   c. beware   f. before

Page 74

a in fair	ar in car	or in store
square	argument	orchestra
dairy	large	important
stare	partner	force
ordinary	guarding	before
area	article	ordinary
January		
dictionary		
daring		
beware		

1. argument   6. dictionary
2. beware   7. article
3. partner   8. before
4. orchestra   9. ordinary
5. important   10. daring

Page 75
These words should be circled:
stare   area
partner   daring
article   argument
orchestra

These words should be circled and written correctly:
1. (fource) (garding) (orkestra)
   force guarding orchestra
2. (inportant) (artikle) (Jenuary)
   important article January
3. (Bewair) (argumints) (lawrge)
   Beware arguments large
4. (areeu) (sqware)
   area square

Page 77
1. equator, different
2. compare, other
3. algebra
4. happen, again
5. puncture
6. quiet
7. lecture, quarter
8. second, thousand or dozen
9. animal

Page 78
algebra   other   dozen   region
thousand   happen   animal   again
along   quiet   second   puncture

1. a bout   10. punc ture
2. oth er   11. thou sand
3. com pare   12. qui et
4. hap pen   13. al ge bra
5. a long   14. dif fer ent
6. re gion   15. e qua tor
7. quar ter   16. doz en
8. sec ond   17. a gain
9. lec ture   18. an i mal

Page 79
These words should be circled and written correctly:
quiet   animal   region
lecture   about   different
equator   punctured   happen
along   seconds   again

Page 81
1. a. athletes   c. children
   b. watches   d. chocolates
2. a. purchases   b. watches
   c. exchange
3. rhythm

4. (thought)   athletes   truthful
   (though)   rhy(th)m   toge(th)er
   ari(th)metic   mon(th)s   leng(th)

Page 82
1. awhile   10. purchases
2. thought   11. though
3. exchange   12. friendship
4. rhythm   13. length
5. chocolates   14. white
6. watches   15. children
7. where   16. arithmetic
8. athletes   17. months
9. truthful   18. together

1. months   4. chocolates
2. athletes   5. watches
3. children   6. purchases

These words should be circled:
women   people

Page 83
These words should be circled:
athletes   together   awhile
length   though   exchange

These words should be circled and written correctly:
1. (atheletes) (munths)
   athletes months
2. (childrn) (arithmutic)
   children arithmetic
3. (perchases) (choclates)
   purchases chocolates
4. (frendship)
   friendship
5. (exchan) (waches) (wite)
   exchange watches white

Page 85
Down   **Across**
1. bridge   3. electric
2. generous   6. dangerous
4. regular   8. signals
5. country   9. peaceful
6. decided   12. genius
7. since   15. energy
10. circle   16. concert
11. figure
13. segment
14. nice

Page 86

1. g	9. k
2. j	10. s
3. j	11. s
4. g	12. k
5. j	13. s
6. g	14. s
7. g	15. s, k
8. j	16. k, s

1. coun try	7. danc ing
2. sig nal	8. gen ius
3. peace ful	9. dan ger ous
4. seg ment	10. gen er ous
5. fig ure	11. e lec tric
6. cir cle	12. reg u lar

Page 87

These words should be circled:

dancing   regular   figure
signal   country   electric
segment   energy   genius
          concert

These words should be circled and written correctly:

1. cuntry   pieceful
   country   peaceful
2. dangirous   brige
   dangerous   bridge
3. genrous   sinse
   generous   since
4. dansing   cirkle   concirt
   dancing   circle   concert

Page 89

1. terrible, eagle
2. instrument
3. several, celebrate
4. Address, label
5. telescope
6. whole, little
7. example
8. declare, special

Page 90

1. eagle	6. whole
2. towel	7. several
3. special	8. label
4. example	9. little
5. legal	10. terrible

---

1. spe — quent
2. ques — dress
3. fre — clare
4. in — tion
5. de — cial
6. ad — stead

1. special
2. question
3. frequent
4. instead
5. declare
6. address

7. ex — ri — ble
8. sev — e — al
9. ter — e — ple
10. cel — am — brate
11. tel — stru — scope
12. in — er — ment

7. example
8. several
9. terrible
10. celebrate
11. telescope
12. instrument

Page 91

These words should be circled:

special   celebrate
question   telescope
address

These words should be circled and written correctly:

1. Sevral   terible
   Several   terrible
2. eegle   teleskope
   eagle   telescope
3. towle   speshul
   towel   special
4. uddress   lable
   address   label
5. qwestion   insterment
   question   instrument

Page 93

1. a. weigh
   b. their
   c. piece
2. e
   d
   f
   a
   c
   g
   b

Page 94

long **a**	long **e**	long **i**
weigh	piece	tried
	receive	trying
	field	writing
	neither	tired
	siege	

---

1. receiving—drop **e**
2. writing—drop **e**
3. having—drop **e**
4. trying—no change
5. received—drop **e**
6. worried—change **y** to **i**
7. planned—double final consonant
8. hurried—change **y** to **i**

Page 95

These words should be circled and written correctly:

trying   fierce   siege
fields   neither   piece
Their   having   worries
tired   writing

Page 97

1. a. teacher   d. biologist
   b. actor   e. assistant
   c. liar
2. honestly   exactly
   speedily   happily
3. c
   d
   a
   e
   b

Page 98

1. darkness
2. loneliness
3. weakness
4. happiness
5. honestly
6. angrily
7. friendly
8. speedily

1. sad ness	5. exact ly
2. teach er	6. lie ar
3. happy ly	7. lonely ness
4. kind ness	8. act or

Page 99

These words should be circled:

kindness   teacher   honestly
exactly   sadness   happiness
biologist   darkness   speedily

These words should be circled and written correctly:

1. (lyer) (honistly)
   liar honestly
2. (teecher) (frindly)
   teacher friendly
3. (biologest's) (assistent) (speedyly)
   biologist's assistant speedily
4. (happyness) (espeically)
   happiness especially
5. (acter) (exacly) (darknes)
   actor exactly darkness

Page 101

Across	Down
1. byte	2. through
4. principal	3. clothes
10. reign	5. chute
11. heir	6. principle
12. sub	7. hour
14. scene	8. cruise
16. aloud	9. write
17. they're	13. bell
18. isle	15. crews

Non-spelling words are **sub** and **bell**

Page 102

1. scene
2. reign
3. through
4. they're
5. cruise
6. principal
7. write
8. heir
9. aloud
10. hour
11. two
12. byte
13. isle
14. knew
15. chute

long **a**	long **e**	long **i**
reign	scene	byte
		isle
		write

long **o**	**ow**	**oo**
clothes	aloud	through
	hour	cruise
		knew
		chute
		two

Page 103

These words should be circled and written correctly:

(seen) (principal) (close)
scene principal clothes
(threw) (our) (too)
through hour two
(cruise) (principel) (Their)
crews principle They're
(crews)
cruise

Page 105

1. b   6. f   11. k
2. l   7. i   12. d
3. e   8. g   13. m
4. a   9. n   14. j
5. c   10. h

Page 106

1. careless   4. useless
2. excitement   5. government
3. thoughtful   6. plentiful

1. care(less)   5. a muse(ment)
2. waste(ful)   6. won der(ful)
3. thought(less)   7. ex cite(ment)
4. plen ti(ful)   8. suc cess(ful)

Page 107

These words should be circled:

careless   excitement
thoughtless   worthless
reckless   useful
arrangement

These words should be circled and written correctly:

1. (usless) (carless)
   useless careless
2. (arranjment) (amusmen)
   arrangement amusement
3. (wreckless) (punichmen)
   reckless punishment
4. (goverment) (sucesstul)
   government successful
   (pridikament)
   predicament

Page 109

Across	Down
1. caution	2. no
4. official	3. fiction
6. conclusion	5. constitution
8. sugar	7. musician
12. constellation	9. physician
13. addition	10. patience
14. can	11. tension
15. shoes	15. sure
16. glacier	

Non-spelling words are **no** and **can**

Page 110

1. (sh)oes   7. (s)ugar
2. gla(ci)er   8. posi(ti)on
3. cau(ti)on   9. mi(ssi)on
4. (s)ure   10. fic(ti)on
5. offi(ci)al   11. ten(si)on
6. addi(ti)on   12. pa(ti)ence

/sh/ spelled 6 different ways

1. fic ___ ar   1. fiction
2. sug ___ sion   2. sugar
3. pa ___ tion   3. patience
4. mis ___ cier   4. mission
5. gla ___ tience   5. glacier

1. phy clu cial   1. physician
2. con fi tion   2. conclusion
3. of di sion   3. official
4. ad si—cian   4. addition

Page 111

These words should be circled:

shoes   caution   musician
official   glacier   tension

These words should be circled and written correctly:

1. (shure) (shoos)
   sure shoes
2. (missun) (glasher)
   mission glacier
3. (pacience) (musition)
   patience musician
4. (fysician) (tenshun)
   physician tension
5. (conclushun) (ficshun)
   conclusion fiction
6. (oficial) (possition)
   official position

Page 113
1. a. wrong   c. half
   b. answer   d. listen
2. a. knapsack   b. tonight
3. a. wrong   c. scratch
   b. answer   d. listen
4. unknown
5. a. dough   c. half
   b. island   d. whistle

Page 114
1. wrestle   7. half
2. answer   8. whistle
3. honor   9. tonight
4. climb   10. island
5. talking   11. design
6. knot   12. scratch

1. wrong   5. knapsack
2. unknown   6. knot
3. listen   7. climb
4. limb   8. half

1. wrestle—short vowel
2. scratch—short vowel
3. climb—long vowel
4. listen—schwa
5. half—short vowel
6. answer—short vowel
7. dough—long vowel
8. knapsack—short vowel
9. island—schwa

Page 115
These words should be
circled and written correctly:
island   knapsack   talking
tonight   answer   climbed
limb   knot   dough
scratch   design   wrong
wrestled

Page 117
1. illegible   8. disagree
2. misspell   9. misbehave
3. disappoint   10. illegal
4. rebuild   11. reappear
5. misfortune   12. disappear
6. misuse   13. recover
7. rewrite

Page 118
1. disappoint   5. misunderstand
2. misbehave   6. disappear
3. rebuild   7. rewrite
4. illegal

1. dishonest   4. disapprove
2. disagree   5. illegible
3. illegal   6. disconnect

Page 119
These words should be circled:
recover   dishonest   recall
disappoint   illegal   illegible
disapprove

These words should be circled
and written correctly:
1. rebiuld   misfortunate
   rebuild   misfortune
2. rekall   disconect
   recall   disconnect
3. desapprove   missbehave
   disapprove   misbehave
4. mispell   legible   reright
   misspell   illegible   rewrite

Page 121
Down   **Across**
1. nephew   2. paragraph
3. physical   5. telephone
4. festival   8. few
6. enough   10. pharmacy
7. trophy   11. cough
8. fragile   12. triumph
9. fourth   13. briefly

Page 122
1. paragraph   9. pharmacy
2. few or phew   10. festival
3. trophy   11. cough
4. telephone   12. stuffed
5. enough   13. fluid
6. nephew   14. physical
7. briefly   15. fragile
8. roughest   16. triumph

1. trophy   5. fragile
2. enough   6. few
3. pharmacy   7. triumph
4. fluid   8. briefly

1. trophy, triumph
2. fragile, pharmacy
3. briefly, enough

Page 123
These words should be circled
and written correctly:
trophy   triumph   Friday
nephew   Festival   physical
fragile   Briefly   roughest
enough   fourth   few

Page 125
1. imperfect
2. impolite or improper
3. inactive
4. impatient, unable
5. unaware, impolite or
   improper or inconsiderate,
   uncomfortable
6. preview, prehistoric
7. prefix, incorrect
8. prevent, prejudice

Page 126
1. imperfect   6. prevent
2. prejudice   7. inconvenient
3. incorrect   8. prefix
4. uncertain   9. unaware
5. preview   10. impolite

1. imperfect   7. inconsiderate
2. impolite   8. prehistoric
3. unaware   9. uncomfortable
4. inactive   10. inconvenient
5. ungrateful   11. unable
6. impatient   12. improper

Page 127
These words should be circled:
unaware   imperfect   prehistoric
prevent   prejudice   uncertain
inconsiderate   prefix
inconvenient